FIDEL CASTRO
AND THE CUBAN REVOLUTION

FIDEL CASTRO
AND THE CUBAN REVOLUTION

Corinne J. Naden
and
Rose Blue

MORGAN
REYNOLDS
PUBLISHING

Greensboro, North Carolina

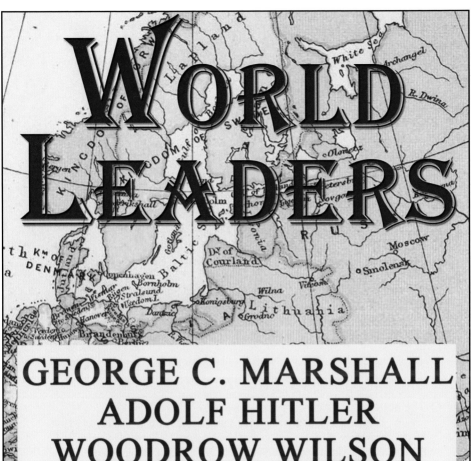

WORLD LEADERS

GEORGE C. MARSHALL
ADOLF HITLER
WOODROW WILSON
VACLAV HAVEL
GENGHIS KHAN
JOSEPH STALIN
CHE GUEVARA
FIDEL CASTRO

FIDEL CASTRO AND THE CUBAN REVOLUTION

Library of Congress Cataloging-in-Publication Data

Naden, Corinne J.
    Fidel Castro and the Cuban Revolution / by Corinne Naden and Rose
Blue.
        p. cm.
    Includes bibliographical references and index.
    ISBN-13: 978-1-59935-029-5 (library binding)
    ISBN-10: 1-59935-029-7 (library binding)
    1. Castro, Fidel, 1926---Juvenile literature. 2. Cuba--History--1959---
Juvenile literature. 3. Heads of state--Cuba--Biography--Juvenile literature. 4.
Revolutionaries--Cuba--Biography--Juvenile literature. I. Blue, Rose. II. Title.
    F1788.22.C3N25 2006
    972.9106'4092--dc22
    [B]
                                                    2006018776

Printed in the United States of America
First Edition

To my longtime writing partner, Rose Blue.
She is greatly missed.

contents

Fidel Castro. (AP Photo)

ONE
A Political Illiterate

Frenzy swept the small island nation of Cuba for a short period in January 1959. From Santiago in the southeast to the capital city of Havana in the northwest, army tanks, local buses, armored cars, and pickup trucks filled the streets and people danced down the city sidewalks and along the country roads.

The cause of the joyous revelry was the overthrow of the hated dictator, Fulgencio Batista, and in Havana some of the revelers took time to bash in the windows of the U.S. embassy and American-owned hotels. They were angry that their powerful neighbor to the north had supplied the dictator with political, material, and military support as the country sank deeper into political corruption.

Two chants sounded throughout the streets during the celebrations. One was "Long live the new Cuba!" The other, "Viva Fidel!" celebrated the hero of the revolution, the young man who had led a tiny band of guerillas to victory over Batista's much larger and better supplied regular army.

When Fidel Alejandro Castro Ruz entered Havana on January 8, 1959, he was dressed in a fresh set of army fatigues, the uniform of the new generation of Latin American revolutionaries. He had only recently emerged from his hiding place in the Sierra Maestra mountain range. He slowly made his way through the throngs of supporters to Camp Columbia, where he addressed a large crowd. As he began to speak, someone in the crowd let loose hundreds of white doves from their cages. When one of the doves lighted on Castro's shoulder, the crowd gasped. Surely this was an omen of Castro's greatness.

Fidel Castro was the undisputed leader of the new Cuba, but his seizure of power would have influence well beyond the borders of his tiny country. It would usher in a new era for the entire Western Hemisphere that has continued well into the twenty-first century.

Fidel Castro, who would grow to be a tall, physically imposing man, weighed twelve pounds when he was born on August 13, 1926. Castro was born on his father's estate, Las Manacas, located in Oriente, a province in the southeastern part of Cuba. Oriente, which means east, and is today known as Santiago de Cuba, was one of Cuba's poorest and most backward areas. It was a province with a few wealthy plantation owners and the many impoverished peasants who worked their land. Education and medical care for the poor workers was limited. Most of the people lived in shacks with no running water or many of the other comforts available in most parts of the Western world.

Fidel did not experience this poverty firsthand. His father, Angel Castro Argiz, owned 25,000 acres of land that produced valuable sugar cane. Castro's mother, Lina Ruz Gonzalez, had started out working as a maid in the Castro household. Angel was Lina's master and a married man, but an affair between the two led Angel's first wife to divorce him. Angel and Lina did not marry until she had given birth to three children, Angela, Ramón, and Fidel. Four more children—Raúl, Juana, Emma, and Agustina—were born after they were married.

Angel Castro's origins were as humble as his second wife's. An uneducated man, Angel had emigrated from Spain to Oriente, where he initaially worked as a day laborer. He was crude, arrogant, hard working, and fiercely ambitious. Over the years he amassed one of the largest estates in the province. Yet for all of his riches, he never shed his peasant background. He dressed simply, always wore a pistol on his hip, and carried a whip even when he walked around the house.

The fact that he was illegitimate probably caused Fidel problems in his early years in Catholic Cuba. But he was the son of a wealthy and powerful landowner, so it is doubtful he was taunted or insulted to his face. Not surprisingly, Fidel knew how to fire a shotgun at an early age and maintained a love for firearms throughout his life. However, he was never close to his overbearing father, who was notoriously tyrannical with the workers on his plantation.

The city of Havana was the center of Spanish-controlled Cuba. (Courtesy of the Granger Collection.)

The sugar industry that was the source of the Castro family wealth had been the backbone of the Cuban economy for hundreds of years. Over the four centuries Cuba was controlled by Spain, it became one of the world's most important sources of sugar. After Christopher Columbus claimed the island for Spain on his first voyage to the New World in 1492, a process of political domination began that eventually killed off or forced most of the native population into slavery. Then, during the eighteenth century, the island's population increased dramatically when slaves were imported to work in the sugar cane fields.

Cuba, which is situated about ninety miles south of Florida, is part of a chain of islands known as the Greater Antilles. It stretches nearly eight hundred miles from east to west, but is only about 119 miles at its widest point, and just nineteen miles at its most narrow. Because of its location and abundant natural resources, European powers used the island as a stopping-off point for explorations into the Americas throughout the fifteenth, sixteenth, and seventeenth centuries.

Revolutions and liberation movements began to sweep through most of the Western Hemisphere nations during the eighteenth and nineteenth century. The increasingly restive populations of countries that had long been colonized by European nations began to fight for economic and political freedom. Cuba began its long struggle for independence from Spain in 1868. The initial conflict, called the Ten Years' War, ended in an eventual stalemate and promises of reform from Spain that went largely unfulfilled.

The United States, which had recently ended its own Civil War and was beginning to emerge as one of the world's industrial powers, closely monitored the situation in Cuba. Even before the Cuban revolt against Spain, many U.S. leaders dreamed of annexing the island. President John Quincy Adams even called Cuba "an apple that had to fall by gravity into the hands of the United States." Spain thwarted a U.S. move to annex Cuba in the middle of the nineteenth century and not long afterward the United States offered to buy Cuba from Spain, only to be denied. Despite these setbacks, Cuba's neighbor to the north kept an active hand in the politics and economy of the island.

The United States had long had a proprietary attitude toward Latin America. In 1823, President James Monroe proclaimed the Monroe Doctrine, which declared that the Western Hemisphere was off limits to further European colonization. President Theodore Roosevelt strengthened the Monroe Doctrine during his presidency in the early 1900s with what came to be known as the "Roosevelt Corollary." Roosevelt said the U.S. would use its influence or military power in Latin America if necessary to abet American commercial interests.

By 1895, U.S. investments in Cuba had reached $50 million, and its annual trade doubled that figure. The United States was the largest and most important buyer of Cuba's sugar crop, although control of the island's economy remained largely in Spanish hands.

In February 1895 another Cuban war for independence

broke out. It was mobilized by the Cuban rebel leader and poet José Martí, who became a national symbol of Cuba's struggle against colonialism. As the war wore on, and news of Spanish atrocities against poor Cubans shocked the world, many Americans began to express sympathy for the rebels and called on the U.S. to intervene on their behalf. Then, in February 1898, the battleship U.S.S. *Maine* exploded and sank while docked in Havana harbor, killing two hundred and sixty American sailors. The cause was never determined, but American newspapers and politicians publicly accused the Spanish government of sabotage. With cries of "Remember the Maine!" U.S. public opinion rallied behind an intervention and war was declared in April of 1898.

With parts of the ship housed at memorials all over the East Coast, some irreverently joke that the U.S.S. Maine *is the longest ship in the Navy.* (Library of Congress)

The Spanish-American War was decidedly one-sided. Spain did not have an army or navy in the area. Commodore George Dewey sailed to the Philippines, where natives were also fighting to overthrow their Spanish colonizers, with his naval squadron on May 1 and destroyed the Spanish fleet anchored there. American troops, including a group of volunteer cavalry led by future president Theodore Roosevelt, defeated the Spanish forces in a battle near Santiago in Cuba, and by December Spain had signed a peace treaty freeing Cuba from Spanish control.

Cuba began its independence during U.S. occupation. The new Cuban government was forced to adopt provisions

This map shows Cuba during the Spanish-American War.

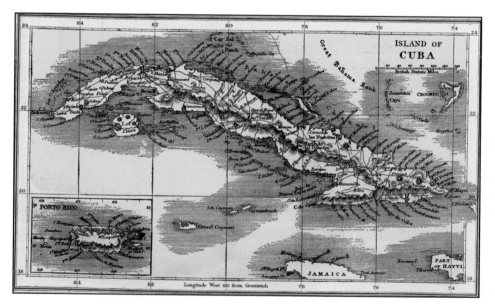

from a U.S. army appropriations bill, called the Platt Amendment, into its constitution. The provisions prohibited Cuba from negotiating treaties with foreign governments other than the United States, allowed U.S. intervention into Cuban affairs when it deemed necessary, and ceded authority of a naval base at Guantánamo Bay to the U.S.

Throughout most of the first half of the twentieth century, a series of U.S.-backed governments ruled Cuba while American companies with business interests in the country prospered. American money poured into hotels and casinos. This unregulated atmosphere inevitably led to political corruption and great imbalances of wealth.

Fidel Castro grew up in a political and social environment of dictatorship, corruption, and civic unrest, but as a child of privilege he was protected from its worst effects. As an adult, he remembered that "because of my father's influence, everyone lavished attention on me, flattered and treated me differently from the other children." He spent his time horseback riding and exploring his father's lands with his friends, who were generally the children of his father's workers. Fidel was a wayward, impetuous child. Once he got in a fight with an older boy who beat him up. Unwilling to accept defeat, Fidel returned three times to fight with the same boy, losing each time. Finally, the older boy conceded victory, just so Fidel would leave him alone.

Fidel began his formal education in a one-room schoolhouse on his father's land, side by side with the children of the laborers. He was a good student, although he often irked his teachers. When he was six, at the urging of one of his exasperated teachers, Fidel's parents sent him to attend La Salle, a school run by an order of Catholic priests in Santiago, the capital of the province. While in Santiago, Fidel lived with his godfather, who was also the Haitian consul. The switch from rich kid on his father's farm to merely one of many students in the big city was a shock for young Fidel. He felt as though his parents had deserted him and was miserable in his godfather's home. He complained to his parents that he was mistreated until they found him on-campus housing.

But Fidel's behavior did not improve. When reports of his troublemaking made their way back to Las Manacas, his father threatened to bring him back to the farm, together with his brothers Ramón and Raúl, who had also entered La Salle. Although Fidel hated the school, he apparently hated the idea of going home even more. Supposedly, he told his father that if he were brought back, he would burn down the family house. Fidel stayed at La Salle.

Fidel was a bright student who rarely applied himself. He later compared the classroom to a prison cell. When his conduct and schoolwork failed to improve, his parents transferred him to the Dolores Jesuit School in Santiago, once again as a day student. He lived in the home of a business acquaintance of his father's. As before, he did not do well in class, although he excelled in sports. He had few close friends and was a self-centered, stubborn, and temperamental young man.

Although an erratic student, Castro took an interest in politics from an early age. He admired the efforts of U.S. president Franklin D. Roosevelt to bring the United States out of the Great Depression that engulfed much of the world economy during the 1930s. When Fidel was fourteen, he wrote a letter to Roosevelt congratulating him on winning a third term. Castro also asked for a ten-dollar bill because he had never seen one. Roosevelt sent back a chatty reply without the ten dollars.

Besides Roosevelt, Fidel's other hero during his school days was José Martí, the Cuban poet and patriot who had led the early stages of the revolt against Spain

At only sixteen years old, José Martí was incarcerated by Spain for his writings against slavery and the Spanish dominance of Cuba. His efforts on Cuba's behalf took him to Spain, France, Guatemala, and the United States. (Courtesy of the Granger Collection.)

Fidel, with a lollipop, while attending Dolores College at age thirteen. (AP Photo)

that eventually led to independence. Martí's name became a synonym for liberty throughout Latin America. In April 1895, he had gathered the support of Cuban exiles in the U.S. and began an invasion of Cuba. He died at the battle of Dos Ríos, on May 19, 1895. Fidel studied the life of this Cuban hero and in later years identified himself with Martí as a fighter for independence.

Despite his mediocre academic work, Fidel was intellectually curious and had a photographic memory. When he encountered a subject he did not enjoy studying, he would simply memorize entire pages from a textbook in order to pass the test. As an adult he has been known to remember specific details from conversations he had years before and can speak for hours without referring to notes.

After Fidel graduated from Dolores in 1942, at the age of fifteen, he was sent to Havana to attend Belen Jesuit Preparatory School, the school of choice for elite Cuban young men. Students wore mandatory uniforms and regularly attended mass. Castro's sister Angela, now eighteen, moved to Havana with him, not for schooling but to care for her favored brother, as was custom. They rented rooms in a boardinghouse, and Angela's duties included taking care of her brother's clothes and making sure he was presentable at all times. Still pampered and used to being the center of attention, Fidel, who was now over six feet tall and weighed nearly two hundred pounds, demanded that his shirts be of the highest quality and ironed precisely to his liking.

When Fidel entered Belen, Cuba was ruled by Fulgencio Batista, who, like Fidel, hailed from eastern Cuba and had even worked on Angel Castro's estate at one point. When he was only a sergeant, Batista had taken part in a 1933 military coup that toppled the regime of Gerardo Machado. Batista soon became prominent in Cuban politics and was the de facto leader of the country behind several puppet presidents until he was elected president himself in 1940. Although corrupt, Batista was a popular president during his first term. He established several government-sponsored public works projects, expanded the education system, and ultimately had the provisions from the Platt Amendment removed from the Cuban constitution. When Batista's term as president ended in 1944, he left Cuba to live in Daytona Beach, Florida. Not yet concerned with politics, Fidel took little interest in Batista's presidency. He later called himself a "political illiterate."

Fidel was now sixteen years old. Although likeable and friendly, he was essentially a loner. Fidel's family was prestigious in Oriente, but Belen was full of the offspring of Cuba's finest families. They knew how to dress, how to act, and how to talk. The boy from Las Manacas did not fit into the social scene at Belen. He was a good baseball player and was named the country's outstanding student-athlete in his senior year.

Fidel's time at Belen left a lasting impression. The Jesuits are known for their freethinking but rigorous academics and they instilled a strong sense of discipline in him. In later years, he said, "I feel that creating habits of discipline and study was good. I am not against that kind of life, spartan to some degree. And I think that, as a rule, the Jesuits formed people of character." He also credited the Jesuits with his appreciation for social justice and honor. When Fidel graduated from Belen in 1945, his yearbook entry read:

> 1942–1945. Fidel distinguished himself always in all subjects related to letters. A top student and member of the congregation, he was also an outstanding athlete, always courageously and proudly defending

The Castro brothers line up for a snapshot at Dolores College. From left to right, Fidel, Raúl, and Ramón Castro. (Courtesy of the Granger Collection.)

the school's colors. He has won the admiration and affection of all. We are sure that, after his law studies, he will make a brilliant name for himself. Fidel has what it takes and will make something of his life.

TWO

Student Revolutionary

Castro decided to study law at the University of Havana. He earned high marks in his studies and began to take an interest in university politics. He was elected class representative to the university government during his freshman and sophomore years. Life on campus at Cuban universities during the late 1940s was largely controlled by student gangs called "action groups." They claimed an interest in university activities and social reform, but acted more like hoodlums. Murder and violence were not uncommon on campus. This tumultuous political atmosphere on the campus closely modeled Cuban politics in general and proved to be a good training ground for Fidel.

The gangs even influenced national politics. Batista's successor, Dr. Ramón Grau San Martín, sought to purge Batista's influence in the military and labor unions and

Founded in 1721, the University of Havana is one of the oldest universities in North America. The school's volatile atmosphere gave Fidel practice in the arts of political wrangling.

enlisted the support of student gangs. He rewarded them with government jobs. Grau's four-year term was bloody. There were over sixty political assassinations, many carried out by student groups that also threatened further violence, rigged the grading system and controlled the market on school textbooks.

Castro, who had inherited his father's ambition, was soon caught up in university politics. He began to speak at political rallies and discovered he was a gifted public orator. The extent of Castro's involvement in the violent student gangs is a matter of some debate. He was close, at different times, to both of the two major rival gangs, the Revolutionary Socialist Movement (MSR) and the Revolutionary Insurrectional Union (UIR).

As Castro became comfortable as a speaker and leader, he began to project an image as a serious-minded young man interested in political reform. He cut a distinctive figure on campus. Tall and handsome, he generally wore a dark suit and tie, in sharp contrast to his more casually attired peers. He did not drink or dance—unusual for a Cuban male—and had few close friends.

As Castro became more involved in campus politics, antigovernment leaders and the press started noticing him. Meanwhile, his awareness of the ills afflicting his country and its people deepened. He became convinced there was too much corruption in Cuba's government, and too little attention paid to the needs of the people. He began to blast President Grau and his policies at political rallies, making him a target for Grau's government agents. It was a dangerous time. Castro would later claim that he faced more danger as a student leader than he did as a guerrilla in the Sierra Maestra. He began to carry a revolver with him at all times.

Initially, Castro's university politics were not overly ideological. He was more interested in projecting his personality into debate and in laying the groundwork for a political career after graduation. But he gradually became more grounded in left-wing politics. While landowners and American investors basked in wealth, most ordinary Cubans were forced to live in abject poverty. Castro became convinced that the only solution was to institute a reform program that would more evenly redistribute land and wealth among the people.

Castro began to admire Eduardo Chibás, a reform-minded congressman of Grau's own party, the Auténticos Party. Chibás wanted a government that would be dedicated to personal freedom and to raising the standard of living for the Cuban people. The personable, enthusiastic Chibás lambasted the government in speeches on the radio and at rallies for its corruption, inefficiency, and disregard for the needs of the people. During Castro's sophomore year in 1947, Chibás announced the formation of a new party called the Orthodoxos Party. Castro was one of the first to join and remained a devoted member for eight years.

Castro did not return home that summer. He joined a group through his university contacts that was getting ready to go and overthrow the government of the Dominican Republic, led by Rafael Leónidas Trujillo. Castro saw the journey as an idealistic campaign to overthrow a corrupt and brutal dictator, and also a way to cement relations with the MSR, which was leading the expedition. Castro's family traveled to Havana to try to talk him out of the idea, but Castro, having now shed the dark suit for the army fatigues and combat boots that would become part of his legacy, was determined.

It was an unprofessional group that assembled for the invasion of the small nation on the island of Hispaniola. MSR leaders Rolando Masferrer and Manolo Castro (no relation to Fidel) led the quasi-military expedition of about one thousand followers, mostly Dominican exiles, mercenaries, and members of Cuban student action groups.

Trujillo had been trained for combat by U.S. marines, who had occupied the Dominican Republic from 1916 to 1924. He quickly rose through the ranks of the military and took over his country in a military coup in 1930. The Dominican people paid for a measure of peace and prosperity under him by forfeiting all civil and personal liberties. Castro thought that the situation in the Dominican Republic paralleled what was happening in his own country.

The Cuban invasion group sailed in three boats from Holguin in Oriente province to the small barren island of Cayo Confites off the coast of Campagüey province. There they trained for the mission while battling with mosquitoes under the blistering sun.

After all the planning, the invasion never happened. When Trujillo heard about it he contacted the United States government, which in turn contacted Grau, who had initially authorized the expedition, possibly in an attempt to get rid of some of the more troublesome dissidents in his own country. Under U.S. pressure, Grau sent a ship to retrieve the would-be invaders. On the return trip, Castro, fearing arrest, jumped overboard and swam to shore in his full uniform and with his gun, through what he described as "shark-infested waters." He was close to his hometown and showed up at the family estate "dripping wet," according to his sister Juana.

Later that year, during a political rally, a high school student was shot and killed in Havana. Castro was one of the thousands who, in protest, accompanied his coffin to the Presidential Palace. In an impromptu speech, Castro attacked the corruption and oppression of the Grau government. His speech roused the crowd of angry protesters.

Over the next several months, Castro became known to fellow students and activists as well as to the Havana police. In February 1948, he was suspected of being on the scene when the MSR leader Manolo Castro was murdered by machine-gun fire. The police questioned Fidel but did not charge him with a crime.

Two months later, Castro was once again in the midst of violence, this time in Bogotá, Colombia. He was with his friend Rafael del Pino attending a student conference sponsored by Gerneral Juan Perón, dictator of Argentina. Most of the students at the conference admired Jorge Eliécer Gaitán, the popular leader of the Liberal party in Colombia. Gaitán reminded Castro of his mentor, Eduardo Chibás, the charismatic leader of the Orthodoxos in Cuba.

On April 9, Gaitán was murdered and a mob lynched the murderer. In the three-day rioting frenzy that followed, known as the "Bogotazo" (the sack of Bogotá), as many as three thousand people died. Although Castro's role remains unclear, he did take an active part in trying to organize the rioters. "It's incredible, truly incredible, that we weren't all killed," he said later. The Cuban ambassador in Bogotá arranged for Castro and del Pino to be flown back to Havana.

When Castro returned from Bogotá, he began campaigning for Eduardo Chibás and the Orthodoxos in the upcoming 1948 election. He traveled the country with Chibás and often spoke before him at political rallies.

Eduardo Chibás gained young Castro's support because of his outspoken denunciation of corruption. In modern Cuba, however, Chibás's name cannot be spoken since he was also ardently anticommunist. (Latin American Studies)

Castro was bitterly disappointed when Chibás lost the election to Carlos Prío Socarrás, the Auténtico candidate who had been Grau's minister of labor. Chibás had failed to organize a grassroots campaign and also did not have the backing of the United States. Though many Cubans resented the United States, most saw their support as necessary in order to get anything done.

Two days after the election, Castro was married. During his time at the University of Havana, he had met and fallen in love with a twenty-two-year-old philosophy student named Mirta Díaz Balart. She was the daughter of a wealthy family from Oriente who disapproved of the marriage. Castro's father, however, was delighted with the prospect of being tied to an important family and threw a celebration.

The newlyweds spent their three-month honeymoon in the United States, first in Miami, Florida, and then—after Castro ran out of money and pawned his expensive watch—in New York City. Castro loved New York, especially the people's fondness for its baseball teams. He took an English-language class and even considered studying at Columbia University.

Castro's marriage turned out not to be a happy one, mostly due to his preoccupation with politics. The couple was always short on money, especially after the birth of their only child—Fidelito—in 1949. One time, their furniture was hauled away and their electricity was often cut off. Angel had to frequently bail them out.

Castro had not finished school, but his time was increasingly filled with political matters. He spent long hours at meetings and often brought home political friends to continue their discussions into the night. He had made many Communist friends and was often in close contact with their officials, although he never joined the party. He was a loyal Orthodoxo.

Theoretically, communism is a system of government in which all property is owned by the state and the people share the common wealth according to need. The goal is a classless society. Communism was originally conceived by the German philosopher and political economist Karl Marx, who argued that the capitalist, or free market, system invariably leads to inequality and exploitation. In 1848, Marx and his collaborator Friedrich Engels published *The Communist Manifesto*, a pamphlet urging the workers of the world to rise up in rebellion and take control of the means of production.

Marx's work was very influential in the twentieth century. In 1917, a Marxist disciple with the underground name Vladimir Lenin seized power in Russia. Lenin and his followers, called the Bolsheviks, executed the Russian royal family and renamed the country the Union of Soviet

Bolshevik revolutionary Vladimir Lenin is mythologized during the 1917 revolution in Russia in this painting from the school of Soviet socialist realism. (Courtesy of Art Resource.)

Socialist Republics (USSR). Lenin was also a writer and a theorist who elaborated on the ideas of Marx, arguing that since revolutions are unlikely to occur organically, they have to be organized and executed by a group of trained revolutionaries.

Marx and Lenin influenced Castro's political thought when he was a student, but it is uncertain how much. The Orthodoxos were not Communists. Chibás railed against communism, as did many of the politicians of the day. Association with communism was seen as a dangerous political liability.

The end of World War II had added another layer to U.S. interest in Latin America. An intense rivalry developed between the U.S. and the Soviet Union that became known as the Cold War. The U.S. saw itself as the steward of capitalism and private enterprise; the USSR championed the worldwide spread of communism. Armed with vast stockpiles of nuclear weapons, the two superpowers staked out spheres of influence and jockeyed for strategic position. Most international diplomacy of the era was viewed through the lens of the Cold War.

Castro finally earned his law degree in 1950, after cramming for the final exams and memorizing page after page of text, and opened a small law firm in a poor section of Havana with two of his classmates. His aim was to work for Cuba's poorest citizens, but Castro was never fully comitted to his new practice. Politics occupied his every thought.

Increasingly, Castro attached himself to Chibás, who,

despite losing the 1948 election, continued to gain public attention with his weekly radio speeches in which he charged the government with corruption. He was poised for another presidential run in 1952. But any hopes for a Chibás presidency were dashed in 1951, after a strange tern of events led to Chibás's death. Chibás, after apparently being fed false information, accused Prío's minister of education of stealing public funds. When the minister accused him of lying and challenged Chibás to produce evidence, the Orthodoxo leader, during one of his weekly radio broadcasts, admitted that he had no proof but insisted the charges were true.

Then he did something bizarre. After recounting his political career and calling on the people of Cuba to "rise up and walk," Chibás, to the horror of those in the radio station—including Castro—pulled out a .38 caliber pistol and shot himself in the stomach. The high drama of this event was lost on the radio audience because his microphone had already been turned off. Chibás died from an infection eleven days later.

Some have speculated that Chibás, who prided himself on his unflinching integrity, could not bear the humiliation of having his word questioned. But if he really intended to kill himself, why not aim at his heart? Most likely it was a dramatic stunt intended to arouse public support. Chibás had also shot himself in 1946 and gone on to win an election as a senator in the Cuban legislature.

Whether or not Chibás intended to die, his death caused an outpouring of sympathy for the Orthodoxos. Castro thought the time seemed ripe to run for public office and decided to run for the House of Representatives. Even though other Orthodoxo party members refused to throw their full support behind him because of his connection to the student action groups, he launched an energetic campaign and looked likely to win.

His party was also poised for victory. Polls indicated that the people favored the Orthodoxos' Roberto Agramonte, Chibás's replacement, for president over Prío. The only other noteworthy candidate was Fulgencio Batista, the former leader of Cuba. But the election never took place.

Out of power since 1944, Batista had lived for a time in Miami in luxury. In 1952, he decided on another bid for the presidency and returned to Cuba. Months before the election, a group of mainly junior officers from the Cuban army, disgusted with the rampant corruption of Prío's regime, approached him about staging a coup. At first Batista refused because he thought he would win the election anyway. But as Election Day neared, he found he was stuck in third place behind Agramonte and Prío. When the officers told him they were going to go ahead with the coup with or without him, he agreed to lead it.

In the early morning hours of March 10, 1952, Batista and several officers, quietly and without bloodshed, took over the huge army barracks at Camp Columbia, where about half of the Cuban army was housed. The operation was a complete surprise; no Cuban troops anywhere opposed Batista. The coup was complete before most Cubans were out of bed. Most accepted the seizure of power quietly.

One of Batista's first acts after regaining power was to dissolve the congress and call off the election. Within weeks, the United States recognized the new regime and began selling Batista arms. Batista had a number of allies in Cuba and in the early days was able to co-opt several potential opposition groups, including the Cuban Communist Party and a number of business leaders and labor unions. The Authénticos and the Orthodoxos both spoke out against the coup but discouraged violent resistance.

One person who did not accept the takeover quietly was Fidel Castro. He later claimed that, had he been elected, he would have worked to reform the government from inside. His hopes of effecting change from inside the government were dashed, but his ambition still burned. Anyone close to Castro knew that he would never accept defeat once his mind was made up. He renounced the electoral process and reasoned that if Batista could wrest control of the government by force, so could he.

In truth, Castro had begun to distrust democratic elections during his days as a student. Both Grau and Prío had been elected democratically, yet corruption, violence, and gross inequality had plagued their presidencies. It was best to take power by force, which would allow him to radically alter the direction of the government without the burden of holding elections.

Castro set about organizing a secret army of revolutionaries through his contacts with the Orthodoxos. He began his movement with a small group of personal friends, including a young, married society woman, Natalia "Naty"

Revuelta, with whom he had been having an affair. By the end of the year, Castro claimed about 1,200 adherents to his movement.

By the summer of 1953, Castro had a plan to oust Batista. He and his conspirators bought a two-acre farm near the city of Santiago de Cuba and began having arms shipped there in bags labeled "chicken feed." Castro planned to lead a troop of one hundred and sixty insurgents in attacking the nearby Moncada Barracks, the second largest army installation in the country. The idea was to take the barracks, steal the weapons stored there, distribute them to like-minded rebels throughout the country, and rally support for a popular rebellion based in the Oriente province. Castro asked his father for $3,000 to help fund the assault, but Angel only gave him $140. His younger brother Raúl also joined the effort. Before Castro and some two hundred of his revolutionaries set off from Havana, he called his mistress Naty to tell her good-bye. He did not call his wife.

THREE

"History Will Absolve Me"

The July 26, 1953, attack on Moncada Barracks was a disaster. Most of the insurgents had no idea what they were doing or where they going. Castro had never been inside the barracks and did not even have a map. When a number of his men rushed into what they thought was the ammunitions armory, they found themselves instead in the barbershop. Only a few of Castro's men died in the attack, but about half were tortured or executed after being captured.

Castro and some of his men fled to the mountains but were soon captured by an army patrol. The standing order was to kill Castro but the lieutenant heading the patrol happened to know him from the University of Havana. He whispered to Castro, "Don't say who you are or they will kill you," and then brought him back alive and handed him over unharmed to the civilian authorities.

At his trial, Castro served as his own lawyer. He held the entire courtroom captive as he argued and gesticulated in his flamboyant oratorical style. He invoked José Martí and the other heroes of Cuban history. The police, who realized Castro was swaying public opinion, forced doctors to report that he was sick and could no longer attend the trial. A guard claimed at the trial that he had been ordered to poison Castro's food but had refused.

On the final day of his trial, however, Castro was allowed to speak. His closing argument was one of his most famous and galvanizing speeches. He spoke for hours, scarcely mentioning the charges leveled against him, but instead railing against Batista. "I do not fear the rage of the miserable tyrant who took the lives of seventy of my comrades," he defiantly said. "Condemn me. It does not matter. History will absolve me!" After this dramatic declaration, there was silence. The people were uncertain whether Castro had finished until he said, "Well, I finished. This is all," and sat down.

In spite of his stirring defense, Fidel, along with his brother Raúl and others involved in the attack, received thirteen years in prison at the Isle of Pines, the nation's largest penal institution, which was located on a remote island south of Cuba. The future looked bleak for the fledgling revolutionary, but if the lengthy sentence bothered him he did not let on. Upon being reunited with his fellow "Moncadistas" (the name the participants of the Moncada Barracks assault gave themselves), he reestablished himself as their leader. Castro did not suffer physically at the Isle of Pines. Political prisoners were treated much better than the other inmates. He had plenty of time on his hands, and read voraciously. He was especially fond of the political writings of Marx and Lenin, but decided that political philosophies change as circumstances do. Pragmatism and flexibility were essential ingredients in any effective political ideology. He continued to admire Franklin Roosevelt.

Castro spent his days shaping future plans. He even worked to elaborate on his "History will absolve me" speech, which would later become something of a manifesto for the Cuban revolution. His friends made copies of it and distributed them as pamphlets to students

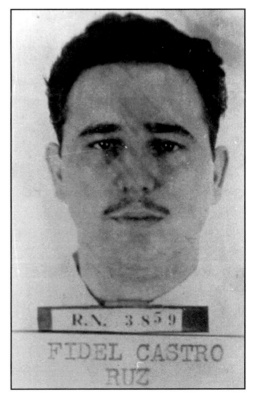

Castro, during his imprisonment on the Isle of Pines after the failed Moncada barracks attack in 1953. (Government of Cuba)

and intellectuals all over the island. It outlined a series of revolutionary principles, which included restoring the constitution of 1940, agrarian reform, and the seizure of land and money from corrupt government officials. But it did not mention communism, and did not criticize the United States or threaten more imminent attacks on the government. Castro had managed not to offend anyone who could potentially be an ally, and his popularity grew as people began to see the Moncada Barracks attack as a brave and defiant gesture against Batista's corrupt government.

Castro's relatively comfortable prison life was jolted in February 1954 when Batista paid a visit to the prison. As the general and his entourage paraded by Castro's ward on their way to the dedication ceremony of a new power plant, Castro instigated the men to shout taunts and sing a revolutionary song. Outraged, the prison authorities threw Castro in solitary confinement for forty days.

Several months later, Castro, while listening to the radio one day, learned that Mirta had lost her job at the Interior Ministry. The loss of employment did not bother Castro, but the fact that his wife had been working for Batista's government certainly did. Adding insult to injury, Mirta divorced him in December and received custody of Fidelito. In a letter from prison, he said the entire affair caused "a new, unknown and terrible sadness."

But good news arrived on May 7, 1955 when Batista declared a general amnesty for political prisoners. Eight days later, Castro, along with Raúl and his followers, walked out of prison after having served less than two years of his sentence.

Fulgencio Batista held sway over Cuba in one way or another for twenty-six years. His agreements with American businesses eventually made Havana the third-wealthiest city in the world. Yet his tenure also saw widespread poverty and corruption. (Library of Congress)

The move was not a display of good will on Batista's part. Things were not going well for the dictator. The previous November, he had held general elections, but no one had dared to run against him. The rigged elections showed seventy percent voter turnout for Batista. The amnesty was his way of saying he no longer had anything to fear from Castro's ragged band.

In truth, Castro seemed to be the least of Batista's problems. The country's economy—especially the sugar industry—was depressed. Although a great deal of U.S. money poured into the country, most of it went into oil refineries, hotels, and casinos and did little to aid Cuban agriculture or general industry, much less the lot of the poor.

Castro returned to Havana as a hero. Except for growing a mustache and gaining a few pounds, he had changed very little during his time behind bars. He made public speeches, boldly proclaiming his intention to free Cuba from oppression and told reporters that his campaign against the government was to be known as the July 26th Movement, in honor of the failed attack on the barracks at Moncada. He also claimed that the government was staging bomb attacks all around the country to justify a crackdown on political dissidents.

It was not long before Batista realized freeing Castro had been a mistake. Batista's administration threatened to shut down newspapers and journals that printed Castro's speeches and jailed those who supported him too loudly. Fidel's brother Raúl was accused of a bomb attack and fled to Mexico City, where many Cuban revolutionaries were already gathered.

Finally, even the unflappable Castro had to get away. Before following Raúl into exile in July 1955, he made contacts with other rebels he hoped would help him when he returned to Cuba. The leaders of the MSR agreed to merge with the July 26th Movement. He also met Frank País, a young schoolteacher and influential dissident leader from Santiago de Cuba, whom Castro appointed as the head of the July 26th Movement's urban action groups.

Upon leaving, Castro wrote a famous open letter to the press:

I am leaving Cuba because all the doors of peaceful

struggle have been closed to me. Six weeks after being released from prison I am convinced more than ever of the dictatorship's intention, masked in many ways, to remain in power for twenty years, ruling as now by the use of terror and crime and ignoring the patience of the Cuban people, which has its limits. As a follower of Martí, I believe the hour has come to take our rights and not beg for them, to fight instead of pleading for them. I will reside somewhere in the Caribbean. From trips such as this, one does not return, or else one returns with the tyranny beheaded at one's feet.

Castro was also leaving behind his son, Fidelito, and his mistress Naty, who was pregnant. He told Naty that he would marry her if she came with him, but she declined. "She had her chance but she missed the train," he said later.

After meeting Raúl and other Moncadistas in Mexico City, Castro began working to win converts. One of the first to join him was the Cuban-born Colonel Alberto Bayo, a one-eyed veteran of the Spanish Civil War. Bayo agreed to train a small guerrilla force, even though he expressed doubt the invasion would work. The revolutionaries leased a ranch about twenty-five miles outside the city, where Bayo conducted training and military exercises.

Guerrilla warfare operates by using small, mobile battle units without a front line. Unlike in traditional warfare, where soldiers launch frontal attacks, guerrillas avoid direct confrontations, harassing the enemy until they can marshal enough military strength to defeat it outright. Tactics involve constantly shifting the base of operations as well as the use of sabotage and terrorism.

It was in Mexico City that Castro met the man who would become one of his most important allies, a twenty-six-year-old Argentinean doctor named Ernesto Guevara de la Serna, who was known by the nickname "Che" (South Americans often use the interjection "che," which is similar in meaning to the English terms "pal" or "buddy," when meeting a friend). Che, like Castro, came from a privileged family, but after training as a doctor and traveling throughout Latin America, became an ardent Marxist-Leninist. In 1953 he traveled to Guatemala with the intention of joining the progressive regime of President Jacobo Arbenz. But a 1954 invasion force, which was backed by the U.S. Central Intelligence Agency (CIA), overthrew Arbenz and installed a military government. Che fled to Mexico City. The experience convinced Che that the U.S. would always oppose leftist governments in Latin America.

When Castro and Che first met, they sat up all night talking about politics, economics, and revolution. Castro invited Che to join his movement as a doctor, and Che accepted. As they trained, Che also proved to be an adept soldier and guerrilla leader. The two men became close as they planned for the invasion of Cuba. They were inspired by each other's idealism, although Che was, generally speaking, the more radical of the two.

Castro needed money to finance his invasion. He traveled the eastern coast of the United States to win financial

Twenty-two conspirators in front of a government building in Mexico City. Fidel Castro is the tall man to the right of the woman in the white dress. Che Guevera is seated on the ground, second from the left. (AP Photo)

support from exiled Cubans. He had modest success, and when he returned to Mexico City he approached Orlando de Cárdenas, a wealthy Cuban and supporter of former president Prío, about buying arms. De Cárdenas was initially leery of Castro, whom he associated with the violent student groups of his university days, but Castro eventually won him over. "He has such a convincing power," de Cárdenas recalled. "When he puts his hand on your shoulder . . . ten minutes later you are saying yes to everything."

Castro needed to move quickly. Rumors of the invasion had made their way back to Cuba, and some of the nation's leaders and businessmen, who feared the instability that an invasion would cause, had formed a group called the Society of Friends of the Republic (SAR), dedicated to a peaceable solution with Batista. Castro knew that the success of his revolution depended on the people being angry with Batista and unhappy with his rule. Any compromise would dampen support for armed uprising.

Batista had connections with the Mexican authorities and in June 1956 the Mexican police arrested Castro. Days later they raided the ranch and arrested forty-five of his compatriots. All were charged with conspiring to overthrow a foreign government and with illegal possession of firearms. After bribing himself and his men out of prison, Castro had the rebels' armory, which had been stored at de Cárdenas's house, moved to the house of Teresa Casuso, a Cuban exile and widow who was sympathetic to Castro's cause. Staying with Casuso was a beautiful eighteen-year-old girl named Isabelle Custodio, whose parents were on vacation. Castro visited the house often, ostensibly to check on the arms, but actually to see Isabelle.

Castro was desperate to leave Mexico before he was deported, assassinated, or arrested again. He was also eager to get the invasion underway before other opposition groups forced him out of the picture. He arranged a meeting with an old enemy, Carlos Prío Socarrás, who had beaten Chibás in the 1948 election and whom Batista had deposed. Prío was living in exile in Miami, and Castro, who had been flagged as a Marxist revolutionary by U.S. authorities, had to enter the country illegally. He joined a group of Mexican oil refinery workers taking a swim in the Río Grande, on the border of the U.S. and Mexico, and swam over to the U.S. side, where one of his men was waiting for him. At their meeting, Prío agreed to give Castro $50,000 in hopes Castro would topple Batista. He probably thought Castro would be incapable of governing. Castro used the money to buy a weather-beaten 85-foot-yacht called the *Granma*, after the grandmother of its previous owner, an American doctor. It needed a good deal of work to be seaworthy.

In August 1956, Castro met with Frank País in Mexico City. País urged him to delay the invasion, arguing that his forces on the island were not ready to lead an uprising, and the Cuban people would not respond to calls for an all-out revolution. But Castro was determined. He also met with José Antonio Echeverría, the leader of a powerful new student group called the Revolutionary Directorate (DR). Castro viewed the DR dubiously. He did not want other groups undercutting him once the revolution began, and

Echeverría was not willing to cede authority to Castro. The two men established a tentative pact that agreed on the goal of overthrowing Batista.

As his men prepared the *Granma*, Castro was distracted by several personal crises. He had asked Isabelle to marry him and she had accepted, but now was asking him to abandon his plans and to stay with her in Mexico. Eventually, she married someone else. When Castro found out, he sat down on a bed in Teresa Casuso's house and said that he had only one real fiancée—the revolution. Around the same time, Castro received word that his father had died. He instructed de Cárdenas, who had broken the news to him, not to tell the other men, and then never spoke of it again.

On the night of November 25, in the pouring rain, Castro and his men made the final preparations to the *Granma*. Melba Hernandez, one of Castro's supporters from the days of the Moncada attack, told him that the rickety ship could not possibly hold more than a dozen men. "I wouldn't deceive you," Castro responded. "About ninety are going." Then he shook her hand and said, "It's time." The men loaded arms, food, and medical supplies and set off into the Straits of Florida.

FOUR

The Revolution

Space was so limited on the *Granma* the seasick men
had to take turns sitting down. Their nerves were soon
so frayed that a few hours after setting sail they became
convinced the boat had sprung a leak and threw some of
their supplies overboard, only to discover that a faucet had
been left on. Days later, a man fell overboard and they
circled for hours before rescuing him.

After a week they arrived cold, wet, hungry, and two
days late on the shore of Playa de los Colorados. The
landing of the *Granma* in Cuba was supposed to coincide
with a series of strikes and protests around the country
organized by Frank País and other urban leaders, but the
invasion force was late and the protests had been violently
put down.

Soon after landing, a patrol boat spotted the party on

The journey of the Granma.

shore, began firing on them, and alerted the armed forces. Having lost the element of surprise, Castro decided to forge inland and take cover in the mountains. Hungry and bedraggled, the men set up camp on December 5 in a sugarcane field at Algría de Pío. At 4 AM, Batista's forces ambushed the rebels. Bombs and heavy fire rained down on the makeshift camp, sending guerrillas scattering in every direction. Many were killed, captured, or fled. When the attack ended, only about twenty rebels remained, including Castro, Che, and Raúl.

Castro gathered the remaining men and made a rousing speech predicting the imminent overthrow of Batista's government. "Now we're going to win," he told them. After

Two of Castro's most avid followers during his time in the Sierra Maestra mountains, his brother Raúl (left) and friend Che. (AP Photo)

this piece of bravado, the guerrillas disappeared into the misty Sierra Maestra to regroup. Slowly, they came into contact with other rebels and peasant sympathizers, and began to build support with the local population. Their group swelled with new recruits.

In the mountains, Castro met Celia Sánchez, an assistant to Frank País. Celia and Castro probably became romantically involved, but she was more important as his loyal assistant. She followed on their treks through the Sierra Maestra, kept records, and managed the rebels' finances. Women often played a surprisingly active role in the revolution. Castro even created a unit of all-women soldiers, despite the objections of some of the men.

Castro imposed strict discipline on his troops and the small group soon became tough and resilient. The guerillas lived rustically. It was difficult to shave, so they grew beards. Castro's long, bushy beard would later become a trademark. Their forced marches and climbing in the mountains made them strong and they soon became familiar with the terrain.

On January 14, 1957, Castro scored his first military victory, as twenty-seven guerrillas charged a remote army post at La Plata. The rebels came away with a machine gun, rifles, food, and medicine and a great boost in morale. Several days later, they ambushed a government patrol that had followed them into the jungle at Arroyo del Inferno. They began to establish a system of attacking, retreating, waiting, and ambushing. Against such elusive tactics, Batista's army, though they were heavily manned and armed and had a full air force, could not mount a decisive attack.

In these and subsequent battles, Castro insisted that the enemy be treated humanely and be given medical attention. He also demanded that rebel forces pay for all the food they took from peasants. This distinguished the guerrillas from Batista's often brutal and corrupt troops.

Soon after the attack on Las Platas, Castro's group discovered a traitor in their midst. Eutimio Guerra was a peasant guide for the rebels who was captured by Batista's forces early on. Guerra showed the army where the rebel camp was set up and then offered to rejoin their group and assassinate Castro for $10,000. After returning, he told Castro he was cold and needed to share his blanket. He lay awake all night holding a gun up to Castro under the blanket, but did not dare shoot for fear of being killed by Castro's bodyguards. Several days later, an air attack targeted their camp with eerie precision and Guerra was caught with a safe conduct pass from the Cuban military. He confessed and was executed by Che.

In February, Castro received a boost from an unexpected source. American journalist Herbert Matthews was a senior editor for *The New York Times* who traveled to the Sierra Maestra posing as a wealthy landowner looking to buy a plantation, and interviewed Castro for several hours. Castro was at his most charming in the interview, coming across as a vibrant, nationalistic—not Communist—leader. He led Matthews to believe that his movement was bigger and more powerful than it really was by having the same group of men marched through the camp several times, each time with different uniforms and disguises, during the interview. Castro also alluded to "other camps" that did not exist. Most importantly, the interview confirmed that Castro was still alive, although Batista was claiming his troops had killed him. When Batista called the story a hoax, the *Times* printed a picture of Matthews and Castro together.

After the Matthews report, other American reporters flocked to the Sierra Maestra to interview him. He continued to charm, but was vague about his intentions once the revolution was over, and claimed not to have designs on power. Many Cubans began to see Castro as a romantic, idealistic figure fighting against the odds, in the vein of José Martí. Castro's rugged good looks enhanced his charm.

Meanwhile, José Echeverría, the leader of DR with whom Castro had met before setting sail on the *Granma*, was stirring up protests in the cities. On March 13, 1957, the DR staged an attack on the Presidential Palace. Echeverría did not inform Castro and the July 26 Movement of his plans. Echeverría always believed that if Batista were killed, the government would fold. Fifty men stormed the presidential offices, but Batista was not there. Echeverría, meanwhile, took over the radio station and began broadcasting that Batista was dead and urging the people to rise up in rebellion. Echeverría did not know that the palace break-in had failed, or that automatic radio devices had cut off his speech before it reached anyone. He was soon killed by police.

After the palace raid, Batista began to purge the leaders of the resistance in the cities. In July 1957, Batista's troops captured and executed Frank País after a house-to-house search in Santiago de Cuba. His loss was a great shock to the revolutionaries, and angry protesters rioted for three days after his funeral. Another brutal purge of the military followed a failed coup against Batista in September. Many moderate Cubans, who under normal circumstances would not have associated with the rebels, were radicalized by the violence of Batista's regime.

Castro's guerrillas, in the meantime, had enjoyed some significant military successes. In May of 1957, they attacked a garrison at El Uvero. Castro fired the first shot through a telescopic rifle into the barracks. The fighting lasted several hours as Batista's army regrouped and returned fire, but the rebels held their ground until the soldiers surrendered. The attack at El Uvero was Castro's first victory using conventional military tactics. The rebels had shown they could fight like a mature army. A subsequent rout of Batista's forces at Piòa del Agua followed.

The tide of popular support was turning against Batista. The morale of his troops suffered as they endured frequent attacks from Castro's elusive guerrillas. Che began publishing a newspaper from the mountains called *El Cuba Libre* (The Free Cuban), and Castro's men captured a radio transmitter and began a station, "Radio Rebelde" that broadcast antigovernment propaganda. The rebels decried the greed and corruption of Batista and the corrupt politicians that accepted bribes from American mobsters building casinos and hotels. In December 1957, Batista even partnered with the American mobster Meyer Lansky to finance the construction of the lavish Hotel Riviera.

The U.S. had been arming and training Batista's forces for some time, but as his grasp on power slipped, officials in the U.S. State and Defense Departments and the CIA began to consider dropping him. They suspected that Castro was a Communist, but they did not want to continue backing Batista if he could not defeat the rebels. Additionally, Batista was using U.S.-supplied arms against a civil insurrection, in violation of international treaties. In 1958, the U.S. cut off arms sales to Cuba.

Flush from his recent victories, Castro overplayed his hand. He called for a general strike on April 9, 1958, but it failed miserably because of disorganization and a lack of support in urban areas. Castro used the failure to his advantage, however. Ever since his arrival in Cuba, the urban leaders of the July 26th Movement had questioned Castro's role as the overall leader of the revolution. Castro blamed the failed strike on urban leadership and was formally made commander in chief of all revolutionary forces under the auspices of the July 26th Movement.

Encouraged by the strike's failure, Batista made a final push to get rid of the rebel army. In May 1958 he sent seven thousand troops into the Sierra Maestra under the control of General Eulogio Cantillo to fight approximately three hundred and fifty rebels. The battle went on for seventy-six days and in clash after clash the rebels proved themselves superior at fighting in the hills. Each time the rebels won a skirmish, their confidence grew; each time the government troops lost, some defected to the other side.

As the rebels picked up converts and territory, Batista's forces eventually had to pull out of the Sierra Maestra. The defeat was a huge blow. Sensing victory, Castro launched a counteroffensive he hoped would encircle the major urban areas. Troops under Fidel and Raúl remained in Oriente to capture Santiago. Che and another rebel leader named Camilo Cienfuegos led separate columns westward.

By the end of the year, the rebels could count on almost daily victories, and Che's men began blockading Cuban ports. Batista's main backers, Cuban businessmen, began

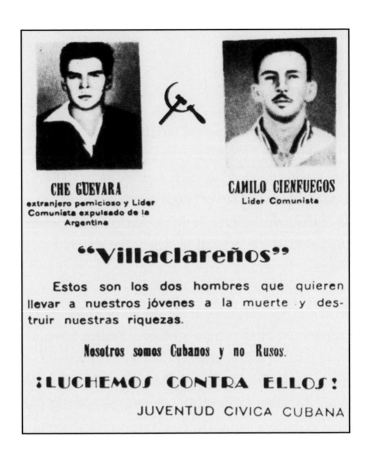

Che and Cienfuegos were wanted men. This 1958 poster reads, "These are the two men who want to bring our youth to death and destroy our wealth. We are Cubans and not Russians. Let's fight against them." (Courtesy of Getty Images.)

to withdraw their support. Former U.S. ambassador William Pawley went to Havana to convince Batista to leave in order to avoid further bloodshed but the dictator refused.

By the end of 1958, however, even the usually confident Batista could see that his time was up. On New Year's Eve, he threw a party at the Presidential Palace. After a meal of chicken and rice, he informed the close friends and officers gathered that he was giving up the fight. Those who wished to go with him, he said, had two hours to get ready. The partygoers scrambled to collect children and valuables. At 2 AM on New Year's Day, the former president and dictator boarded a plane for the Dominican Republic, leaving General Cantillo in charge. Batista eventually went into exile in Madeira, Portugal, and Spain.

Batista's departure caused great rejoicing in the streets, but the country was now without a government. Castro was still in Oriente, and Cantillo and

Castro, speaking after his victory at Santa Clara. The city lay in the path of his march to Santiago. (Courtesy of Getty Images.)

other military leaders were not about to give up power easily. Other potential leaders, most notably Prío, were positioning themselves to seize power amid the confusion and chaos. Castro acted quickly. Over the Radio Rebelde on January 1, he called for a general strike and this time the people responded. The strike turned into a three-day celebration all over the island. Next, Castro ordered Che and Cienfuegos to enter Havana, which they did on January 2, the same day that Castro and his men entered Santiago.

From a balcony of Santiago's town hall, Castro proclaims victory for the Cuban Revolution. Santiago, Cuba's second-largest city, is the birthplace of revolutionary activist Frank País and burial place of Cuban hero José Martí. (AP Photo)

That evening, wearing his grimy, disheveled green army fatigues, Fidel Castro made his first speech as a victorious rebel leader. Filled with historic symbolism and great emotion, the speech praised the Cuban people and promised them that after years of domination and oppression they were now going to carry on the work begun by the martyred José Marti. The victorious rebel leader began the trip westward toward Havana to concentrate the rebel power. In El Catorro, he met up with his son, Fidelito, who had just flown back from Long Island, New York, where he had been sent away to school for the last year of the war.

When Fidel Castro, now thirty-two years old, arrived in Havana on January 8, 1959, the crowds went wild. Smoking a cigar, with his son perched next to him, Castro waved to the crowds from atop a tank as they shouted "Viva Fidel!"

FIVE

The Socialist State

Castro appointed Miguel Urritia, a well-liked judge who had shown sympathy for the rebel cause during the revolution, as president of Cuba. Although Castro remained the head of the rebel army, he seemed content to watch the government proceedings from his suite on the twenty-second floor of the Havana Hilton, built less than a year before with U.S. money. He shared the quarters with his aides and two of his sisters. Security was tight, and the only two people who could visit unannounced were Raúl and Che.

During the first few weeks, Castro apparently toyed with the idea of stepping back and allowing free elections. He even briefly considered leaving Cuba to lead a rebellion against Trujillo in the Dominican Republic. He thought he would not enjoy the business of government as much as he had fighting the revolution. "I miss my mountains,"

Castro's son, Fidelito, flew home from the U.S. shortly after Havana was taken. He was nine years old and had not seen his father for three years. Here, the two bond in Castro's room at the Havana Hilton. (AP Photo)

he told a reporter. As time went on, though, he involved himself more and more in governmental affairs.

Throughout his time as a rebel leader, Castro had dealt with the United States very delicately. He knew that the Americans would intervene if they saw him as a threat to their economic or political interests. The U.S. government had closely followed the developments in Cuba and debates raged in the CIA and State Department over whether or not Castro was a Communist.

Castro was able to avoid answering the question for the time being, but he made other missteps in the early days that put him at odds with the United States. Outside of his hotel one day, as a crowd of admirers and several reporters greeted him, he was asked what he would do if the U.S. were to invade Cuba. He responded with characteristic bravado, "Yes, I tell you, two hundred thousand gringos will die if the United States sends marines to Cuba." The offhand remark upset many government officials in the United States.

Castro faced another dicey dilemma in the issue of justice for former Batista officials. Many Cubans who had been persecuted by Batista clamored for retribution. Castro agreed that many of the accused were murderers and criminals who needed to be punished. At the same time, excessive brutality could cause international outrage. Castro put Che and Raúl in charge of meting out punishments. The trials showed some semblance of integrity, and some of the accused were acquitted, but the judgments were generally harsh and muddled. The walls of the La Cabaña fortress in Havana soon echoed every night with the sounds of firing squads.

After the secret courts received criticism, Castro held some of the trials at a soccer stadium. Large crowds attended the proceedings and shouted taunts at the accused. They cheered for death sentences and booed defense

Time Magazine's *January 26, 1959, issue. An article, "The Vengeful Visionary," laments the deaths of two hundred condemned counterrevolutionaries.* (Time Warner)

arguments. The entire spectacle struck some in the American press as barbaric.

The new provisional, "official" government found it difficult to get anything done. Everyone looked to Castro for directions. In February 1959, the prime minister, Miró Cardona, resigned, and Castro took his place. He would erratically drop in on Cabinet meetings, make decisions, and leave. For all of his success as a rebel leader, he had no experience running a government. "We were very ignorant of government problems," he later admitted. "That is, we were ignorant about the government apparatus and how it functioned."

While making a television address as prime minister, Castro received news that Fidelito, who was living with his mother in Havana, had been in a serious jeep accident. Instead of rushing to the hospital, Castro continued talking for some time. Raúl eventually convinced him to wrap it up, and when he got to the hospital, a furious Mirta upbraided him. "You haven't changed," she shouted. "You are irresponsible as usual."

In late February, Castro was invited to the United States by the Society of Newspaper Editors. He arrived on April 15 with an entourage of about seventy people to speak in Boston, New Jersey, and Central Park in New York City, where thousands showed up. Castro described his idea of the Cuban Revolution: "No bread without liberty, no liberty without bread; no dictatorship by one man, no dictatorship by classes, groups, castes. Government by the people without dictatorship or oligarchies; freedom with bread, bread without terror: that's what humanism is all about." He spent much of his time fending off questions about his Communist leanings.

Castro was popular with the American press during his trip. He joked with reporters and shook hands with crowds. With New York policemen guarding his every move, he visited the Bronx Zoo, spoke at the United Nations, took the elevator to the top of the Empire State Building, and met baseball hero Jackie Robinson. Castro has always had an affinity for baseball, which he played as a youth at Belen.

Castro's U.S. trip was a public relations success,

but not a diplomatic one. President Dwight Eisenhower conveniently left Washington when Castro came to visit, although the Cuban leader did meet with Vice President Richard Nixon. Nixon aggressively questioned Castro and later reported to Eisenhower and the State Department that Castro was probably a Communist. Castro later said of Nixon, "Sincerely I never liked Richard Nixon. From the first moment I could see he was a false man. He always hated our country." Castro left the U.S. feeling snubbed by the Eisenhower Administration.

Back in Cuba, Castro set about the business of governing. He envisioned a total transformation of Cuban society, in what he called a "humanist revolution." One of his first priorities was agrarian reform. A new law set limits on land ownership, with exceptions for foreign companies that served the national interest. Castro's family estate at Las Manacas was one of the first properties seized during agrarian reform. The reforms, which were relatively moderate, were mostly drawn from recommendations by the United Nations Commission on Latin America. Castro set up the National Institute for Agrarian Reform (INRA) to oversee expropriation and redistribution of land, as well as health care, transportation, education, and housing policy.

Castro also focused on consolidating his political power. Reporters pressed him about holding elections, which he likely would have won in a landslide, but he resisted. Castro did not intend to hold elections that might distract attention from his reforms and embolden his critics to attack his plans. He worked long days at the INRA and turned

Castro implemented many land reforms in an effort to redistribute wealth and property and to bolster Cuba's flagging economy. This poster reads, "To Camagüey Province, with the faith and valor of the Moncada fighters." (Courtesy of the Granger Collection.)

it into the main arm of the Cuban government. He also began replacing old-guard politicians, including President Urrutia, with revolutionaries loyal to him.

Urrutia had become a liability when he began criticizing the influence of Communists in the new government. In protest, Castro abruptly resigned as prime minister and then went on television to accuse Urrutia of being a pawn of U.S. interests. Urrutia was powerless without the support of Castro and even before Castro had finished speaking he had offered his resignation to the Cabinet. A little more than a week later, Castro returned to his post as prime minister and appointed a loyalist named Osvaldo Dorticos as president.

Urrutia's concerns about Communist influence in Cuba were not unfounded. Although most mainstream politicians shunned the Cuban Communist Party (even Castro had kept his distance in the past) they had an extensive grassroots political network and enjoyed significant support among peasants and the urban underclass. Castro began to see the advantage in courting Communists and appointed many to high positions. Though neither Che nor Raúl were members of the Communist Party, they were both committed to Marxist ideology and exerted enormous influence on Castro.

As Castro moved further to the left, he faced dissent from within and outside the country. U.S.-based Cuban exiles began bombing raids in Pinar del Río and wealthy landowners resisted land seizures in the Camagüay Province. When Che and Raúl began a campaign to recruit more leftists into the military, a veteran of the revolution named Huber Matos resigned from his post as a military commander in the rebel army and called for Castro to rid his ranks of Communists. Castro had him arrested, tried for treason, and imprisoned for twenty years at the Isle of Pines, the same prison that had held Castro after the Moncada attack.

The chief of staff of Castro's air force, Pedro Díaz Lanz, also protested Communist influence in the government. He defected to the United States and later detailed Castro's links to communism in testimony to a Senate committee. The same day Matos was arrested, Lanz flew a jet over Havana dropping pamphlets that called for the removal of all Communists from the Cuban government. Castro only hardened his resolve against what he called "counterrevolutionary activities."

Shortly after Batista's overthrow, Castro established a network of local committees across Cuba called the Committees for the Defense of the Revolution (CDRs) designed to report and suppress political opposition and other allegedly subversive activities. CDRs kept tabs on people's spending, work, and personal habits, and reported any suspicious activity. Throughout the 1960s, they were often used to persecute artists, intellectuals, and homosexuals.

Castro occasionally revealed his inexperience as a leader and could seem to be more interested in retaining power than in his country's welfare. Ernesto Betancourt, an economist from the Ministry of Finance, described a meeting where several economic advisers warned Castro of the danger of a U.S. intervention. Castro responded, "Well, I couldn't care less, because if that were to happen, if they were to send the marines, they would have to kill three or four hundred thousand people and I would get a bigger monument than José Martí." Several months later, the president of the national bank resigned and Castro replaced him with Che, who had no experience in finance.

Castro's harsh "counterrevolutionary" measures also alienated many liberals who came to see Castro as simply another despot. Although he still enjoyed popular support, a number of upper- and middle-class Cubans began to flee to the United States. Many ended up in Miami and became fierce opponents of Castro there. The exodus also led to a shortage of trained professionals in Cuba. Universal health care was one of the revolution's main goals, but many of those who left were doctors.

Castro's behavior toward the United States also grew increasingly erratic. During the agrarian reform program, Castro had nationalized land belonging to several U.S. companies. When U.S. officials complained about the seizures and asked him to compensate the companies, he responded by seizing the remainder of American plantations. U.S. officials generally associated this type of behavior with communism.

But nothing alarmed the United States more than Castro's increasing friendliness with the Soviet Union. In February 1960, Soviet Vice Premier Anastas Mikoyan visited Cuba and signed several trade agreements, as well as a $100 million loan. In May, the two countries formally established diplomatic relations. Although he knew the United States would be infuriated by a Soviet ally so close to its shores, Castro needed the security and economic backing.

Castro's view on the Soviet Union was complicated. He did not want to become a Russian pawn in the Cold War. While still fighting in the Sierra Maestra, he had told Raúl, "I hate Soviet imperialism as much as I hate Yankee imperialism. I am not breaking my neck fighting one dictatorship to fall into another." But as tensions developed between him and the U.S. leadership, the Soviet Union's support became more critical. Castro accelerated his land, health, and education reforms in an effort to appease the USSR and ramped up his attacks against the United States in his public speeches.

Though Castro's antagonism toward the United States may have endeared him to the Soviets, it was poorly timed to electoral politics in the United States. Castro and the Cuban revolution became a prominent issue in the 1960 presidential election campaign. The Republican candidate, Vice President Richard Nixon, and the Democratic candidate, Senator John F. Kennedy, competed over who would be tougher on Castro. As the current vice president, Nixon was at a disadvantage because he could not criticize Eisenhower for being soft on Castro, leaving Kennedy free to ratchet up the rhetoric. Kennedy openly talked of overthrowing Castro and accused the Eisenhower Administration of doing nothing.

However, the CIA under Eisenhower had developed a number of covert, anti-Castro plans. There were several assassination plots in the works, as well as attempts to publicly embarrass him in some unusual ways. The CIA even considered dusting his shoes with thallium, which would cause his beard to start falling out. Another alleged plan involved lacing his cigar with poison. The Eisenhower Administration is widely rumored to have asked American Mafia boss Sam Giancana to assassinate Castro. The mob, which had flourished in Cuba under Batista, had reasons of its own to want to see Castro dead. Over the years, Castro has claimed that there have been over six hundred attempts on his life by the American government. The CIA has acknowledged only five.

Most significantly, however, the CIA set up camps in Miami and Guatemala to train an invasion force of anti-Castro Cuban exiles. The invasion was modeled after the successful CIA-organized scheme to overthrow Jacobo Arbenz in Guatemala in 1954. Although Castro did not know the specifics of these plans, Castro anticipated a U.S.-sponsored invasion and stepped up his efforts to enlist Soviet aid.

In September 1960, Castro traveled to the U.S. for a United Nations conference in New York. The trip was relatively uneventful, but Castro met Soviet Premier Nikita Khrushchev for the first time. Khrushchev was like Castro in many ways—energetic, brash, cunning, and wildly unpredictable. When a Phillipine delegate at the conference criticized Russia's position on imperialism, Khrushchev brandished his shoe and pounded it on his desk while calling the delegate a slew of insulting names.

Castro at the United Nations conference in New York. (Library of Congress)

Later that year, a string of events increased tension between the U.S. and Cuba. In June, a shipment of Russian oil arrived in Havana and Castro instructed three U.S. oil companies in Cuba to refine the oil. When they refused, he had them nationalized. In retaliation, President Eisenhower stopped Cuban sugar shipments to the United States. Khrushchev agreed to buy the sugar instead and Eisenhower shot back by banning almost all U.S. exports to Cuba. On January 3, 1961, the U.S. formally cut off relations after Castro made a speech proclaiming his intention to expel all but a handful of diplomats from the U.S. embassy in Havana.

John F. Kennedy had been elected president of the United States in November 1960. Shortly before he assumed office, Kennedy learned of the CIA's secret invasion plans. Although he had serious misgivings about the plan, Kennedy's anti-Castro campaign rhetoric had boxed him in. After talking tough he could not back down now without losing face. He decided to go forward with the CIA's plan.

Kennedy wanted the attack to look like an internal, civil rebellion against Castro, not a U.S. intervention. He had a force of B-26 bombers disguised with Cuban air force insignia. On April 15, 1961, they bombed airfields at Camp Colombia, San Antonio, and Santiago de Cuba, wiping out much of Castro's air force, although it was obvious the attacking planes were not from Cuba's air force.

The second wave of the U.S.-led invasion came two days later, when fifteen hundred mostly Cuban armed men, who had been trained by the CIA and called themselves the Liberation Army, landed at Playa Girón on the Bay of Pigs. Castro personally led a group of soldiers that swarmed to the landing site and pinned down the invasion force. The invasion was bogged down as the Liberation Army awaited reinforcements and air support that never came. Confusion turned to fear as Castro's army closed in.

The mission had been poorly planned in Washington. The troops who had trained in Guatemala had been

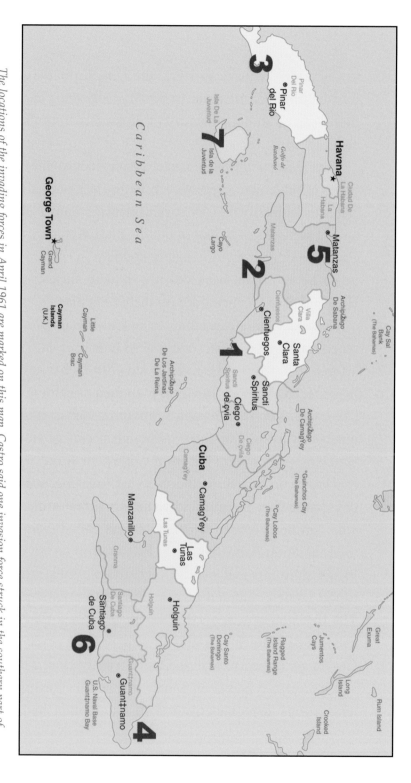

The locations of the invading forces in April 1961 are marked on this map. Castro said one invasion force struck in the southern part of Las Villas Province (1). Another force was reported ashore at the edge of southern Matanzas Province in the Cochinas Bay area (2). Other reported landings took place in the Western Pinar Del Rio Province (3), Baracoa (4), in the Matanza Province (5), and the Santiago area (6), with parachutists dropped on the Isle of Pines, now called the Isle of Youth (7). (AP Photo)

mostly former pro-Bastista exiles and members of Castro's new government who had defected. The two groups did not get along and neither group was inclined to take up arms with the very people they had just fought during the revolution. The CIA had planned for the Liberation Army to move quickly to a close mountain range. Instead, they chose the Escambray Mountains, over a hundred miles away, for cover. They promised the fighters that fellow sympathizers would join them in Cuba, but none arrived. They promised air cover, but the president had not authorized any. Despite the success of a first air strike, an indecisive President Kennedy did not order a second wave, which was even more important because it was to come after troops had landed. With no air support, the mission was doomed.

The invasion crumbled a mere five days after it landed. The Cuban Army killed one hundred and fourteen Liberation Army soldiers and took prisoner another twelve hundred. Castro used the prisoners for both propaganda and ransom. The cost to the U.S. was staggering; the four billion-dollar budget for the invasion swelled to 46 billion. The U.S. eventually had to buy the prisoners' release for $62 million in medical supplies.

The failed Bay of Pigs invasion was an enormous embarrassment for the CIA, the United States, and President Kennedy. It was also a political boon for Castro. If he had not already been the people's hero, he certainly was now. He had succeeded where so many Latin American leaders had failed; he had defied the U.S. His popular support and international standing soared.

At the height of his popularity, when no one would dare question his authority, Castro further consolidated his power. He called off elections and rounded up thousands of political prisoners. He was also free to move as far to the left as necessary to please the Soviets. He began calling the Cuban Revolution a "socialist revolution" (rather than a "humanist revolution," as he had called it before) and declared, "I am a Marxist-Leninist, and shall remain a Marxist-Leninist until the day I die."

Castro now claimed that he had been a Communist all along, and had simply hidden his true beliefs to gain power. This is unlikely, however. In 1965, a U.S. journalist asked Castro if he would sign a piece of revolutionary money he had bought in Havana in 1958. Castro said, "You better not let anyone in the United States know you contributed to a Communist revolution." The journalist replied that he did not know the revolution was going to be Communist when he bought the money. Castro laughed. "You know something," he said, "neither did I."

In January 1962, Pope John XXIII excommunicated Castro on the basis of a 1949 papal decree denouncing Communist governments. Cuba is predominantly Catholic and the move was designed to weaken Castro. Though Castro was strongly influenced by the Jesuits, he has not been a practicing Catholic since he was a child and claims to be an atheist. Castro retaliated by closing a number of seminaries, expelling some foreign priests, and censoring church publications. But after a few years, an unspoken compromise evolved. If Church leaders refrained from criticizing Castro, he would leave the Catholic Church in Cuba alone.

Castro's swing to the left also helped to marginalize the importance of the old-line leaders of the Cuban Communist Party. He wanted to make sure that the Soviets did not try to bypass him and deal directly with the official party. He wanted to do things his way. Before the revolution, when Castro was still an Orthodoxo, he had joked with his Communist friends that he would join the Communist Party, but only if he could be Stalin—the total dictator. Now, he could essentially do just that—join the Party and immediately assume his place atop the leadership.

Even at the height of his political power, Castro did not indulge in the excesses that characterized many other Latin American dictatorships. He traveled constantly, involving himself in various projects to stay in touch with the people. When average Cubans appealed to him for help, he often granted their wishes. Once during the early 1960s, a young woman told Castro that her fiancé was a political prisoner at the Isle of Pines. Castro ordered the man be released, calling it his wedding present to the young woman. He did not hesitate to join laborers in the sugar cane fields. He lived austerely, shunning alcohol, drugs, and gambling. He did enjoy Cuban cigars.

At his side most of the time was Celia Sánchez, the woman who had been his assistant throughout the revolution and continued to handle his affairs until she died in 1980. Celia was an excellent administrator and endlessly loyal. She advised him, controlled his schedule, handled all of his paperwork, and made sure his orders were carried out. The extent of their relationship is unknown, although they almost certainly had some romantic involvement. Whatever his relationship with Celia, Castro had numerous affairs with other women.

Celia, Raúl, and Che, Castro's inner circle, pose at a 26th of July celebration. (Courtesy of Getty Images.)

Castro made universal education one of the pillars of the revolution. He set up literacy brigades and ordered educated Cubans to get out into the country and teach. He would frequently drop by to check on the progress of these campaigns. In the course of one of these visits during the 1960s, Castro met a young schoolteacher from the port city of Trinidad named Dalia Soto del Valle. Little is known about Dalia, but she and Castro were married at some point and had five sons: Alejandro, Alexander, Alexis, Antonio, and Angel. Castro eventually sent Fidelito and his other sons to boarding school in Moscow, although only Fidelito remained in the public eye. Next to nothing is known about his other sons.

Castro's victory at the Bay of Pigs, as well as his renewed hold on political power in Cuba, convinced the USSR that they could deal with him. Khrushchev, who saw Kennedy's actions during the Bay of Pigs as a sign of weakness and inexperience, wanted to seize the opportunity to make a strategic move against the United States. He and other Soviet leaders approached Castro about installing nuclear missiles in Cuba.

The Cubans and Russians haggled over the terms of the deal. The Russians intended to maintain their stronghold over the missiles and troops. Khrushchev insisted they would be used only as a last resort, but this did not satisfy Castro. He did not want Cuba to become merely a Soviet launching pad. Khrushchev agreed to sign an agreement declaring that any attack on Cuba would be considered an attack on the Soviet Union. Even as Raúl wrapped up the agreement in Russia, Soviet cargo ships headed toward Cuba. The world was on the brink of the most dangerous confrontation of the Cold War.

Fully aware that 1962 was a congressional election year in the United States, Khrushchev wanted the missile base to remain a secret until the November ballots were cast. But his plans were thwarted when U.S. U-2 spy planes photographed clear evidence of the missiles. Intelligence officials presented these findings to Kennedy on October 16. The images revealed missiles, tracks and dollies for transporting them, and storage areas.

The range of the missiles varied from 1,300 to 2,500 miles. Apprehension turned to anger in the White House as Kennedy and his advisers pored over the photographs. The Soviets could now launch an atomic attack on any city in the United States from Cuba. The president ordered military commanders to maneuver troops within striking distance of Cuba and to prepare for an invasion.

On October 22, Kennedy appeared on nationwide television and informed the U.S. public of the danger. He described the discoveries made by the spy planes, leaving no doubt that the U.S. now had an enemy missile base less than a hundred miles from its shores. Kennedy then announced the U.S. response. He had initially wanted to impose a military blockade against Cuba, but aides advised him that it would technically be an act of war because it would stop every ship entering or leaving the country. Instead, the president referred to his response to the missiles as "quarantine." The U.S Navy was ordered to circle

Cuba and block any Soviet ship that tried to pass and to board the ships to check for weapons.

Kennedy assured the public that if the Soviet Union launched missiles from Cuba, the U.S. would make a "full retaliatory response." Kennedy's speech raised the possibility of a worldwide nuclear holocaust.

Kennedy's threat rattled Khrushchev, who knew the U.S. had nuclear missiles in Turkey that could target Moscow and other population centers in the Soviet Union. Now he was facing the prospect of nuclear war if the missiles were not removed. He also began to worry he had misjudged the new American president. Kennedy seemed resolute. After Kennedy's speech, Soviet leaders argued furiously about what to do.

Khrushchev delivered his response in a private message to Kennedy on October 26. He agreed to take the missiles out of Cuba if Kennedy pledged not to invade the island and to remove U.S. missiles from Turkey. Khrushchev shortly thereafter made a public speech outlining the same terms.

As the U.S. and Soviet Union tried to find a way out of the situation without losing face, Cuban troops were preparing for an invasion. On October 27 they shot down a U-2 plane, killing the pilot. Kennedy tried to downplay the incident in hopes of reaching a diplomatic solution, although he had refused Khrushchev's first offer. With the Bay of Pigs still fresh in his mind, Kennedy was determined not to appear weak. He dispatched his brother, Attorney General Robert Kennedy, to the Soviet embassy in Washington with a counteroffer. The U.S. would withdraw its missiles from Turkey but would not concede that its withdrawal was conditional upon the Soviets removing their missiles from Cuba. Also, the Russians would have to keep the Turkey compromise a secret or the deal was off.

Khrushchev had little choice. On October 28, he announced the Soviet Union would take its missiles out of Cuba if the U.S. pledged not to invade. Khrushchev's agreement to keep quiet about the removal of missiles from Turkey damaged the Soviet premier's reputation because

The October 29, 1962, edition of The New York Times *heralds the agreement between Kennedy and Khrushchev.* (Courtesy of The Granger Collection.)

it seemed that Khrushchev had simply folded without getting anything in return.

Castro was furious when he learned of the deal. He felt belittled and betrayed; neither Kennedy nor Khrushchev had even acknowledged him as a player in the crisis. Both sides had treated him like a pawn. Khrushchev did not even tell Castro of his decision to remove the missiles. Castro found out, like most people, over the radio. When he heard the announcement, he smashed a mirror and spewed a barrage of swearing and insults at Khrushchev. In a rash move, he publicly insulted Khrushchev's manhood. In later years, however, Castro admitted that Khrushchev's decision to turn back and prevent nuclear war was the correct one. Furthermore, Cuba had not lost entirely after the crisis, for it was officially safe from the threat of a U.S. invasion.

SIX

The Russian Connection

The Cuban Missile Crisis soured Castro's relationship with the USSR, but he could not afford to break with the superpower. He did need to establish some independence from the Soviets, however, and the best way to do this was by exploiting the growing tension between the Soviet Union and another Communist state, the People's Republic of China.

During the reign of Khrushchev's predecessor, Joseph Stalin, China and Russia had a close alliance. The chairman of the Chinese Communist Party, Mao Zedong, supported Stalin when the rest of the world reviled him as a dangerous tyrant. Stalin's reign in Russia was marked by millions of deaths and a number of brutal purges of party officials. After Khrushchev ascended to power he openly denounced Stalin and this alienated Mao, who admired

Stalin and shared his hard-line position toward the United States. During the 1950s China and Russia grew increasingly at odds and competed for the allegiance of other Communist countries. Both wanted to assume leadership of the worldwide Communist movement. This rift became known as the Sino-Soviet split.

One of the issues the two powers disagreed on was whether each country should focus on the revolution within its respective borders or actively encourage it abroad. Although the USSR nominally supported a number of fellow Communist states, it was careful not to antagonize the United States too much by actively stirring up revolution around the world. The Chinese were not as careful to avoid conflict—not if it meant withdrawing support for Communist revolutions elsewhere. After the missile crisis, Castro made overtures to the Chinese by sending Che on a diplomatic mission to China and openly calling for revolutions throughout Latin America. Castro wanted to prove to the Soviets he would not be taken for granted.

The tactic worked and the Soviets began working to mend the relationship. In April 1963, Castro traveled with a diplomatic envoy to the Soviet Union, where he was met with a huge reception and great fanfare. He traveled throughout the Soviet Union, attending banquets and receptions and meeting with Soviet politicians. A stamp was issued in his honor, and he was awarded a Gold Medal for being a Hero of the Soviet Union. Khrushchev assiduously courted Castro's favor throughout his visit. Although his actions during the

During his visit to Moscow, Castro took an unscheduled nighttime walk in Red Square just to fluster his hosts. Here, he and Khrushchev embrace. (AP Photo)

Cuban Missile Crisis had averted nuclear war, Khrushchev seemed to feel guilty about how he had treated Castro and frequently said he thought of Castro as a son.

Full Soviet support strengthened Castro's hand politically. Soviet officials were now giving him approval to run the revolution as he saw fit. Part of Castro's original aversion to communism was that it was too doctrinaire and did not allow for flexibility. Now he could claim allegiance to the Communist cause without actually having to toe the party line.

Upon his return to Cuba, Castro turned his full attention to the revolution. He had initially intended to rapidly industrialize the economy, much like the Soviet Union had done in the 1930s under Joseph Stalin. But the island was short on basic resources and capital. Industrialization required professionally trained workers, many of whom had fled the country. There were such shortages of raw materials and goods that the government had to start a system of rationing. Part of the trouble stemmed from a U.S. economic embargo on all Cuban goods launched by President Kennedy before the missile crisis in February 1962. Castro blamed the U.S. for Cuba's economic woes.

During Castro's trip to Russia, Khrushchev had convinced him that the sugar industry was the backbone of the Cuban economy and offered him a higher price for Cuban sugar. Castro had previously resisted efforts to increase sugar production because the sugar industry was so closely associated with colonialism and imperialism, but he now shifted to a more gradual approach that combined industrial development with agricultural (mostly sugar) production.

In July 1963, Castro's mother died. When he showed up at her wake surrounded by an entourage of intelligence officers, his sister Juana was deeply offended. She considered their presence inappropriate and publicly spoke out against her brother. After a minor scandal, Castro barred the Cuban press from reporting details of his personal life or that of family members. Although still highly visible, he guarded his privacy. He cultivated the popular image that his personal life was the revolution and that he worked around the clock.

As tensions eased after the Cuban Missile Crisis, President Kennedy began to consider reconciling with Cuba. He told Castro, through clandestine channels, that he would be willing to ease up on some measures and to acknowledge that supporting Batista had been a mistake. Castro appreciated this gesture and joked to Jean Daniel, a reporter relaying messages between the two leaders, that "If you see him [Kennedy] again, you can tell him I'm willing to declare Goldwater my friend if that will guarantee Kennedy's reelection." Castro knew that Barry Goldwater, the presumptive Republican presidential candidate, would suffer in the political race if Castro voiced any support for him.

This rapprochement ended in November 1963 when Kennedy was assassinated. Lyndon Johnson, who assumed the presidency upon Kennedy's death, put off plans for future negotiations with Castro. There was even slight speculation that Castro was involved in the assassination, or that members of the Cuban exile community, angry over Kennedy's botched handling of the Bay of Pigs invasion, were responsible.

In early 1964, soon after Kennedy's death, Castro traveled to the USSR again to meet with Khrushchev and to firm up Soviet economic support for Cuba. They signed a five-year trade agreement, and Castro promised not to further provoke the Americans, with whom Khrushchev was trying to repair relations. Castro was willing to ease up in return for economic aid.

After Castro returned home, his promise to Khrushchev was severely tested when the U.S. Coast Guard picked up four Cuban boats with thirty-six fishermen aboard in U.S. waters. The U.S. government ruled that no law had been broken and ordered their release, but the Florida State government imprisoned the men and took the boats. A furious Castro went on television to denounce the action, declaring that the United States violated Cuban waters and airspace every day. In retaliation, he ordered the water supply cut off to the naval base at Guantánamo Bay. The U.S. responded by firing a number of Cuban workers at the base.

The crisis ended when a judge in Florida fined the Cuban boat captains and gave everyone a suspended sentence. The men paid their fines and left for Cuba. Castro, in a generous mood, restored the water to Guantánamo. Later, the naval base set up its own water supply.

Castro was soon faced with a problem with his European ally. In October 1964, Khrushchev was deposed from power in a bloodless coup led by his own right-hand man, Leonid Brezhnev. Khrushchev had been a fatherly figure to Castro. Brezhnev, on the other hand, came across as a stern, bureaucratic leader occupied with consolidating his own power. He left Castro free to conduct foreign policy as he wished, disregarding the agreements Castro had made with Khrushchev not to antagonize the U.S.

Disillusioned with the state of affairs in Russia, Castro began to take an active role in stirring up revolution in Africa. He considered himself more of an anti-colonialist, or "anti-imperialist," as he liked to say, than a Marxist. The nations of Africa have no history of old-line Communist parties, or of entrenched U.S. business interests. The battle for power centered among tribal groups and in an atmosphere of centuries-long European colonialism.

In the early years of his rule, Castro had already shown support for revolutionary movements in several African nations, such as Ghana, where he set up a guerrilla training base in the early 1960s, and Algeria, which was struggling for its independence from France when Castro took over Cuba. In 1960, he sent arms to aid a revolutionary fighter named Ahmed Ben Bella, one of the founders of the Algerian National Liberation Front. Castro also asked for Cuban medical students to volunteer to serve in Algeria. The response was enthusiastic, thus beginning a Cuban program of sending volunteer doctors to Third World countries. Algeria won its independence in 1962 and Ben Balla became its first president. When war broke out between Algeria and Morocco in 1963, Castro sent a few hundred troops to aid Ben Bella.

Castro also saw his efforts in Africa as a way to alleviate a growing problem at home. Che Guevara had been a valuable ally during the revolution and in the early months after seizing power. Castro had been able to use Che's radicalism as a foil to his own moderation. But now that he had declared himself a Marxist-Leninist and expelled or imprisoned most of the moderates, Castro had little political use for Che. In addition, Che was having a hard time adapting to being in power. He was happier fomenting revolt and leading guerillas than working in government. After an ill-fated stint as the president of Cuba's National Bank, Che spent several years as the minister of industry. Castro had made the adjustment from revolutionary to political leader, but Che had not.

There was another problem with Che. He was incredibly popular, which combined with his increasingly vocal political radicalism, made him something of a loose cannon. On several occasions, Che publicly questioned Castro's decisions. Clearly something had to be done.

Castro's opportunity to rid himself of the Che problem came when civil war broke out in the Congo in Africa. Belgium had granted the Congo independence in 1960 but had tried to retain its influence, and became one of the several factions involved in a scramble for power. There were other competing interests as well. U.S. companies mined the mineral-rich land, the Soviet Union saw the opportunity to gain a Communist foothold in Africa, the Congolese military wanted greater power and influence, and the United Nations had interceded to restore order.

In 1960, Patrice Lumumba became the first prime minister of the Congo, and Joseph Kasavubu was elected president. When Moise Tschombe, the head of the copper-rich province of Katanga, tried to break off from the Congo, Lumumba appealed to the Soviets for help, which resulted in his being labeled as a Communist in the U.S. and

By the time Che arrived in the Congo, most of the rebels had given up on their cause. He tried to teach the discouraged men guerilla tactics and they tried to instruct him in the ways of magic. In the end, they valued the revolutionary more for his skills as a doctor than as a fighter and leader of men. (Courtesy of Getty Images.)

Europe. Kasavubu, together with a powerful military leader named Joseph Mobutu, ousted Lumumba in 1961. He was assassinated shortly thereafter. Rebels who had been loyal to Lumumba set up a base in Kisangani, but were driven out in 1964 by Belgian forces backing Kasavubu and Mobutu.

Che, who felt a strong solidarity with the Soviet-backed Congolese rebels, traveled to New York and made a blistering speech to the United Nations assembly. With Castro's encouragement, he renounced his Cuban citizenship and traveled to the Congo in 1965 with a force of 125 Cubans to join the guerrillas. However, despite Che's talent as a military leader, his Congolese campaign was a debacle. The rebels were disorganized and undisciplined, and Che could not get them to obey him. Several months later, he withdrew from combat.

After Che's failure in the Congo, and the overthrow of Ahmed Ben Bella in Algeria in 1965, Castro drew back from his interference in African politics and turned his attention to Latin America. In 1966, he hosted what he called a Tricontinental Congress, during which he continued to play the Russians off the Chinese. His goal was to position himself as a leader in the Third World. Before the conference, he blasted the Chinese for distributing propaganda to the military and cutting off rice shipments to Cuba, a gesture aimed to please the Soviets, who provided Castro with needed economic support. However, during the Congress, Castro openly proclaimed support for armed uprisings around the world, in direct opposition to stated Soviet ideology. He won the respect of leftist leaders throughout Latin America who resented the Soviet Union's lack of commitment to armed revolution in their countries.

Castro also established contacts with revolutionary governments in such countries as Vietnam, Zanzibar, and South Yemen. He vowed to assist any Marxist guerrilla groups that fought the governments of Colombia and Venezuela, both of which opposed the Cuban revolution.

In 1967, Castro established the Latin American Solidarity Organization (OLAS) with a slogan of "the duty of the revolution is to make revolution." In a speech to the delegates at its first meeting, Castro declared that leadership for a Marxist-Leninist drive in Latin America now rested with this new group, not with Moscow. In addition, Castro condemned the Soviet-backed Communist party in Venezuela, known as the PCV, because it no longer publicly supported armed revolution. Castro even sent money and arms to the main guerrilla leader there. It was an open rebuke to the Russians and won Castro great respect in the Third World.

It was this push for revolution in Latin America that eventually took the life of Che Guevera. After his failed Congolese campaign, Che spent some time in Prague, Czechoslovakia before returning to Cuba. In the fall of 1966, Castro encouraged him to lead a group of Cuban guerrillas, this time against the U.S.-backed Bolivian government.

Che arrived in Bolivia disguised as a balding, middle-aged Uruguayan economist named Adolpho Gonzalez. He soon assumed leadership of a small guerrilla band, and spent a year struggling against a Bolivian military trained by a U.S. special forces team. The Bolivian peasants were not as receptive to Che's message of revolution as their Cuban counterparts had been. Che continued to fight bravely, despite overwhelming odds and the harsh jungle terrain. Then, on October 8, 1967, a detachment of the Bolivian army surrounded his group near the banks of the Rio Grande. Che was wounded in the battle and captured. He was executed the next day.

Although Castro publicly mourned Che's death, he used it as a powerful propaganda tool by turning him into a martyr for the revolution. His romanticized figure was soon looking down from billboards on the highway

A crowd in Cuba pays tribute to Che in front of a banner with a quote of his reading: CREATE TWO, THREE, MANY VIETNAMS. (Courtesy of Time Life Pictures/Getty Images.)

and was put on postcards and stamps. His speech to the United Nations was broadcast each year. In his honor, Castro proclaimed 1968 as the "Year of the Heroic Guerrilla Fighter." The Cuban revolution had lost its greatest inspiration, but Castro remained its most powerful force.

Che's death, however, marked a turning point for Castro's support of armed struggle in Latin America. He had been playing a dangerous game. In the period immediately after Khrushchev was ousted, the leaders in Moscow did not know how to handle Castro without alienating their new allies in Latin America. But Castro was reliant on the Soviets for trade, and the leaders in Moscow were tiring of his continued deviance from party ideology and his growing influence in the Third World. They began to criticize Castro through surrogates in Latin America.

Initially, Castro resisted bowing to the Russians. In May 1967, he refused to sign the Nuclear Non-Proliferation Treaty, which was cosponsored by the Soviet Union and the United States and signed by some 189 countries. The treaty banned the pursuit of nuclear weapons except for those countries that had already acquired them. Castro argued that it was merely a maneuver to keep the Third World countries weak.

In December 1967, the Soviet Union held private discussions with Castro in Moscow on economic aid for Cuba. The Soviet leaders apparently threatened to cut off support if Castro refused to curb his behavior. After the meeting Castro dropped his support of armed struggle in Latin America. In August 1969, he made a great gesture of loyalty toward the Soviets and Brezhnev when he appeared on Cuban television to support the Soviet invasion of Czechoslovakia.

Czechoslovakia was a Communist state and a member of the Warsaw Pact, a military alliance that joined Russia and several other Communist-controlled Eastern European states. In early 1968, reformist Alexander Dubcek had taken over the party leadership in Czechoslovakia and eased restrictions on the press and political dissidents. This trend toward liberalization alarmed Brezhnev and other hard-line Soviets. On August 21, 1969, Soviet troops rumbled into Prague. Dubcek and five other party leaders were taken to Moscow for serious talks at which they agreed to end the reforms. When Dubcek returned to Prague, his power was weakened and the progressive trend ended. Brezhnev's action defined what became known as the "Brezhnev Doctrine"—the Soviets claimed the right to intervene in Soviet Bloc countries that were drifting away from communism.

Several Communist parties in the West severely criticized the Soviet action, and most expected Castro to do likewise. It was a classic case of the "Soviet imperialism" he had long spoken out against. But in his television speech, Castro defended the invasion by citing what he said were alarming developments in Czechoslovakia under Dubcek. These included opening talks with the then-West Germans and negotiating for loans from the United States. Under

Dubcek, Castro claimed, the Czech Communist party seemed to be edging toward a working relationship with capitalists and the West.

Whether or not Castro wholeheartedly believed what he said in the speech, he knew Brezhnev was closely watching his reaction to the Soviet invasion. Brezhnev had made it clear he would tolerate no break in Communist loyalty. Castro was also concerned that any sign of strain in the Warsaw Pact might cause the United States to take aggressive action against Cuba.

After Leonid Brezhnev led the 1964 coup against his mentor, Nikita Khrushchev, he remained general secretary of the Soviet Communist Party until 1982. (Library of Congress)

Throughout the late 1960s and early 1970s, Castro became increasingly tied to the Soviet Union. Brezhnev visited Cuba in 1971 as a sign of recognition and approval. Castro needed both. The year before, Cuba failed to meet the ten-million-ton sugar harvest that Castro had predicted. To further strengthen his ties to the Soviets, Cuba formally became a Communist state at the first Communist Party Congress held on the island in 1972. In his address Castro heavily praised the Communist Party and vowed absolute allegiance to party doctrine. This was hardly the talk of the nationalist, independent leader who led the rebels against Batista in the late 1950s.

As Castro began to fall in line with the Soviets on the international stage, he turned his attention to his own country. He put special effort into health care and education and made dramatic increases in the literacy rate. He also poured resources into the health care system, turning it into one of the finest in the world. The overall economy sagged under the top-heavy Communist mandates, but a land reform program significantly improved life for many poor Cubans. Women's rights also improved dramatically.

Although Castro spent most of his time attending to affairs of state, a personal crisis troubled him during this time. In 1956, Castro's ex-mistress Naty Revuelta had borne him a daughter named Alina. He was in exile in Mexico at the time of Alina's birth, and busy waging the revolution and governing Cuba for some time thereafter. Alina did not learn that Castro was her father until she was ten years old. She seemed delighted at the news but, except for a few visits, she saw relatively little of him.

As Alina grew into her teens, she became more rebellious. At the age of seventeen, she announced her forthcoming marriage to a secret police officer many years her senior. Castro summoned her to his office and told her that she was too young to get married. Besides, he said, the man had just separated from his wife.

Alina remained defiant, so Castro struck a bargain with her. Admitting he had not been much of a father, he asked her to wait six months to get married. If after that time she still wanted to go ahead with the marriage, Castro would pay for the reception and attend the wedding. Alina agreed. Six months later, the wedding took place, but it was shrouded in such secrecy that hardly anyone knew about it. At any rate, the union lasted just a few months.

Although Castro's relationship with the Soviets mostly precluded him running an independent diplomacy, he did cultivate relations with other Latin American leaders. In 1970, Salvador Allende, a Socialist, was elected president of Chile. Allende enacted an aggressive reform agenda that bore all of the hallmarks of a leftist government in Latin America: land reform, redistribution of wealth, and expropriation of U.S. assets. Castro had known Allende since his revolutionary days. He visited Chile in 1971 and presented Allende with a gift—a gun with an inscription that read, "To Salvador, from your companion in arms." Less than two years later, Allende was overthrown in a military coup backed by the CIA and led by General Augusto Pinochet, who ruled Chile as a dictator for the next fifteen years. As the military surrounded the Presidential Palace, Allende shot himself with the gun Castro had given him. Allende's death weighed on Castro, but Castro, in his usual manner, did not dwell on the tragedy.

SEVEN

On Behalf of the Poor

Castro's capitulation to the Soviets in the late 1960s and early 1970s eroded his standing in the Third World. In addition to the OALS, Castro had been trying to gain influence within the Non-Aligned Movement—the group of countries not allied with either the United States or the Soviet Union. But after repeated public displays of loyalty to the Soviet Union, he could hardly be regarded as neutral.

Castro began to seek opportunities to expand his influence and assert his independence without offending the Soviets. As he had in the early 1960s, he set his sights on Africa. In 1972, he spent two months traveling in western Africa. In one of his lengthy speeches before his departure, he told the Cuban people that since the threat of an American attack had passed and now that the revolution was firmly in place, he could leave the country without worries. Castro's first stop was Guinea. Formerly a French protectorate, Guinea was made an overseas French territory in 1946. When it gained independence in 1958, Sekou Toure, who had led the liberation movement, became its first president. Like Castro, Toure turned to the Soviet Union for both military and economic support.

Castro felt a kinship to Toure. Both men were very popular in their own countries and both were outgoing and charismatic. On the flight over, seated next to the Guinean ambassador, Castro spent his time reading about the revolutionary situation in Guinea. The two leftist rulers spent five days together exchanging stories and compliments on one another's leadership. They pledged mutual defense if attacked.

The next stop was Algiers, the capital of Algeria on the Mediterranean coast, where the people greeted Castro with much enthusiasm and fanfare. Colonel Hourairi Boumedienne, the country's military leader, met Castro at the airport and held a dinner in his honor. During his speech, Castro did not mention his old friend Ahmed Ben Bella, to whom he had once sent aid. Boumedienne had ousted Ben Bella in a military coup in 1965. At the time of Castro's visit, Ben Bella was behind bars. He was eventually exiled to Switzerland.

In 1974, Castro finally found the perfect opportunity to forcefully reenter the world stage when Portugal, whose new leaders had just dislodged a military dictatorship, announced it would grant independence to its colonies the following year. One of the Portuguese colonies, Angola, located in southern Africa, had three different factions contending for power. Two groups were backed by the United States, and a third—the Marxist-led People's Movement for the Liberation of Angola (MPLA)—by the Soviet Union. The MPLA held the capital city of Luanda, but was foundering because of a lack of Soviet reinforcements.

Castro, who already knew and admired the MPLA leader Agostinho Neto from his earlier involvement with the Congo, decided to send military aid. The USSR, which wanted to see Angola become part of the Soviet Bloc, encouraged Castro, but the effort was his own. He began sending ships with troops, tanks, and heavy equipment and personally supervised every stage of the operation by telephoning instructions and keeping track of troop movements on a huge map in his office.

The United States was displeased with the possibility of Cuban troops aiding the MPLA. President Gerald Ford said that Cuban involvement in Africa would kill any chance for improved relations between the U.S. and Cuba, but Castro was unimpressed. The day after Ford spoke, Castro stood before a crowd in the Plaza of the Revolution. "It's too late," he said. "We don't need them for anything."

Moving so many troops and so much equipment across the Atlantic was a daunting task. At first, most of the troops were sent by ship, but later, when the fighting grew more intense, the Soviets provided huge transport planes. The problem then became one of refueling on the trips from Havana to Luanda. The United States pressured Barbados,

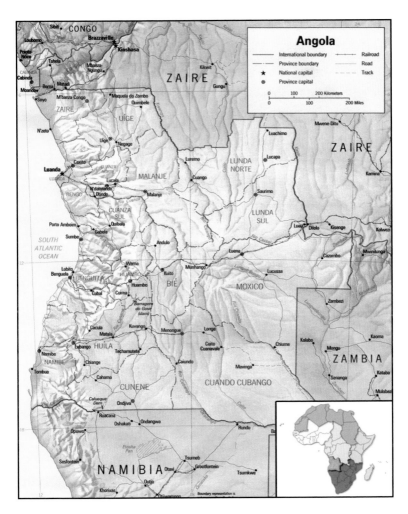

Castro supported the People's Movement for the Liberation of Angola over U.S. protests with both arms and men.

an island country in the Caribbean, to refuse the transport planes' requests to land there for refueling, and the governments of Trinidad, Guyana, and the Azores all denied Cuba's requests for landing rights. The Soviet planes had to pick up supplies in Havana, fly to the seaport town of Conakry in Guinea, and then to Angola.

By January 1976, some 15,000 Cubans were stationed in and around the Angolan capital. The reinforcements fought off attempts by the South African-backed groups to take Luanda, eventually forcing them to beat a hasty retreat back to South Africa. At the time South Africa was controlled by a white government that had imposed a brutal regime of racial segregation called apartheid. A good percentage of the Cuban soldiers were black. Castro intended to portray the war as a struggle against the racist government in South Africa and, by extension, what he claimed was a white supremacist government in the United States. All of Castro's involvements in Africa attempted to foster the idea of a racial connection and heritage between the people of Africa and those of his island nation. "Many of our ancestors came as slaves from Africa," he said. "African blood flows freely through our veins."

Eventually, about 300,000 Cubans—including soldiers, doctors, and humanitarian workers—were sent to aid the Marxists in Angola. Castro publicized the fact that Cuban aid was more than military. In time, the MPLA took control of the government in Angola, and Neto became its first president.

Castro's action in Angola earned him popular support and international acclaim. Many Third World leaders admired his personal loyalty to Neto, in contrast to the U.S. and the USSR, who only sought to expand their influence. In 1976, the Non-Aligned Movement recognized and endorsed Castro's role in Angola and invited him to host the next summit in 1979, making him chairman for the next three years.

Flushed with success over his involvement in Angola, Castro embarked on a long tour of Africa, engaging in talks with another new ally, Muammar Qaddafi of Libya. He spent ten days with the mercurial Libyan leader, even riding through the desert with him and visiting his birthplace. Qaddafi had once mocked Castro's interest in the Non-Aligned movement, but now seemed to be a firm ally, and treated the Cuban leader like a visiting dignitary. The two heads of state swore to defend each other against their enemies. Quaddafi awarded Castro Libya's highest medal, the Bravery Decoration, and Castro praised the Libyan general by citing his "efficiency, dynamism, and courage." He also said, "We came as friends, and we depart as brothers,"

Next, Castro turned his attention to the turmoil in Ethiopia in eastern Africa. Ethiopia and Somalia were in the midst of a border dispute over the region known as Ogaden. This desertlike part of eastern Ethiopia was sparsely populated by Somali-speaking nomads and had long been a source of conflict between the two eastern African neighbors. In September 1974, a group of army officers deposed the longtime emperor of Ethiopia, Haile Selassie and a bitter fight ensued for power. Two years later, Major Mengistu Haile Mariam, who supported a Marxist-Leninist government, emerged as Ethiopia's new leader. Castro immediately sent him a letter of congratulations. As the internal fighting continued, Somalia chose this time to attack and Mengistu appealed to Castro. Once again, Castro sent money and men to Africa and helped the Ethiopians drive the Somalis from the area.

On the heels of his involvement in Ethiopia, Castro scored another political win, this time in Latin America. Since the late 1960s, Castro had been funneling aid and training to the Sandinista rebels in Nicaragua, who were waging a guerrilla campaign against the corrupt Somoza regime. In 1979, the Sandinistas finally seized power and installed a leftist government. Cuba stepped up its aid for the new government.

After Castro hosted the Non-Aligned summit in 1979, he attended the fall session of the United Nations General Assembly, his first in many years. He pointedly spoke for all the nations of the Third World:

> There is often talk of human rights, but it is also necessary to talk of the rights of humanity. Why should some people walk barefoot, so that others can travel in luxurious cars? Why should some live for thirty-five years, so that others can live for seventy years? Why should some be miserably poor, so that others can be hugely rich? I speak on behalf of the children in the world who do not have even a piece of bread. I speak on behalf of the sick who have no medicine, of those whose rights to life and human dignity have been denied . . .

After his U.N. speech, many nations, especially those in the Third World, changed their views of Castro. He seemed to have matured into an important and dignified leader from the scruffy guerrilla warrior he had been two decades before. He became close friends with a number

Castro, giving his impassioned speech to the United Nations General Assembly in New York as the Non-Aligned Movement's spokesperson. (Courtesy of Getty Images.)

of world leaders, including South African anti-apartheid activist Nelson Mandela, who later became South Africa's first post-apartheid president; Indian prime minister Indira Gandhi; Yugoslavian dictator Josip Tito; and even Canadian prime minister Pierre Trudeau. Castro was a pallbearer at Trudeau's funeral in 2000.

By supporting Marxist groups in Angola, Ethiopia, Nicaragua, and Grenada, Castro had managed to find a way to become a hero to the Third World without alienating the USSR, whom he still relied upon for oil and trade. But a few years later, Castro found himself in a position where he had to choose between the two. Afghanistan, in the heart of south-central Asia, was a politically stable country until 1973, when a coup toppled the monarchy. In 1978, a coalition of leftist parties overthrew the new government and began a series of socialist reforms, which met strong popular opposition. Sensing that the new Marxist government was in trouble, the Soviet Union invoked the Brezhnev doctrine and invaded Afghanistan in 1979. They asked Castro to contribute military aid to the cause.

This request presented Castro with a problem. He could hardly afford to turn down a Soviet plea for aid. However, Afghanistan was a member of the Non-Aligned Movement, which Castro supported. By aiding the Soviets he would risk squandering all of the respect he had earned for his involvement in Africa. In the end, Castro decided to risk displeasing the non-aligned countries, and he sent nearly thirty thousand troops to fight. Both the Soviet Union and Cuba were severely criticized for their actions in Afghanistan.

The invasion was a disaster. Afghan guerrillas offered strong resistance, controlling much of the countryside for years, while the Soviets held the cities. The U.S., meanwhile, funneled aid to Afghan resistance groups that fought the Soviets to a bloody standstill. Finally, the Soviets began withdrawing their troops in 1988.

The Afghanistan debacle vexed Castro, but an even bigger blow arrived in 1980 when Castro's personal aide and confidante Celia Sánchez died of lung cancer. Those close to Castro claimed he said it was the saddest day of his life. After Celia's death, Castro sunk into depression.

Before, he had always been an almost ubiquitous presence in his country—bounding around tending to the affairs of government and personally dispensing justice and favors. Now he withdrew from public view. The effect on the government was almost immediately visible. No one felt comfortable doing anything without Castro's consent, yet he was not around to make decisions.

One serious result of Castro's withdrawal and depression happened in the summer of 1980, when a large number of Cubans seeking political asylum took over the Peruvian Embassy in Havana. Perhaps just to get rid of them, Castro relaxed restrictions and announced that anyone who wanted to go to the United States could do so through the port of Mariel. The total number who left turned out to be about 125,000, and most of them were of the working class, the very blue collar people Castro claimed were at the heart of the Cuban revolution.

Shocked and embarrassed that so many wanted to leave, he ordered that a few thousand criminals and mentally ill patients be sent with the dissenters. Soon dozens of boats of every size, jammed to the gunwales, crossed the choppy waters to Key West, Florida. U.S. president Jimmy Carter at first welcomed the influx of Cubans, but soon realized that Castro had seeded the refugees with some of his society's most undesirable people. A U.S. congressman was finally able to convince Castro to stem the flow of refugees. In the end, the entire affair made Castro look foolish, as if he were bitter that the people did not like it in their own country and was childishly taking out his frustration on the

U.S. Some have attributed Castro's botched handling of the Mariel boat lift ordeal to his distraught state of mind over Celia's death.

In 1980, Ronald Reagan was elected president of the United States. Stridently and loudly anti-Communist, Reagan voiced displeasure at the leftist leanings on Grenada, the smallest, poorest, and least known of the Windward Islands in the Caribbean. In 1974, Great Britain had granted independence to this tiny island, known only for exporting nutmeg and mace. But a corrupt government led to a coup five years later led by Maurice Bishop, a Marxist and old friend of Castro's.

Reagan's displeasure increased when he learned that Castro was helping to construct a modern airport on the island. Reagan feared that this airport, hundreds of miles from Havana, would be used as a refueling point for flying Cuban troops and supplies to Africa. Castro aggravated the situation by delivering a series of speeches thundering against the U.S. administration and vowing to stand firm against any interference. When Bishop stopped in Havana to speak to Castro in 1983, he expressed no fears about a U.S. intervention.

Back in Grenada, though, a group of hard-liner Communists thought Bishop's reform agenda was too cautious. When Bishop returned, he was placed under house arrest and later executed in a coup led by General Hudson Austin and Bishop's own deputy prime minister, Bernard Coard. The United States decided to take advantage of the chaos in Grenada. On October 25 Reagan sent in U.S. troops, paving the way for the arrests of Austin and other radical leaders. Cuban soldiers and workers sent by Castro were returned home. U.S. forces gradually withdrew from the island, and a general election established self-government in 1984. Castro praised those who were killed in the fighting and denounced the U.S. action. He also demoted several Cuban officers who had not resisted when the U.S. landed.

But the most troubling developments of all for Castro during the 1980s occurred on the other side of the Atlantic. In 1985, Mikhail Gorbachev became the general secretary

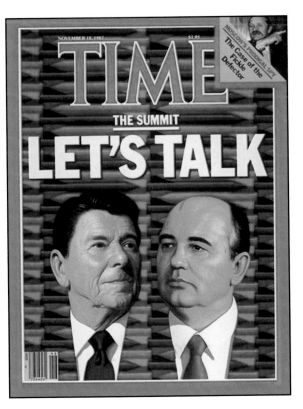

In 1985, Ronald Reagan and Mikhail Gorbachev met at a Geneva Summit. It was the first summit meeting attended by Russian and U.S. leaders in six years. The talks opened the way for a thaw in Soviet-U.S. relations. (Time Warner)

of the Soviet Communist Party and leader of the country. Though he faced some opposition from Communist hardliners who wanted to retrench their position, Gorbachev pushed through a series of reforms he called *Glastnost* (openness) and *Perestroika* (reconstruction). Perestroika was primarily a series of economic reforms aimed to liberalize the economy. Under *Glasnost*, the press was allowed more freedom and there were modest attempts to democratize the political system. Gorbachev also developed warmer relations with both China and the U.S.

After a visit to Moscow in 1986, Castro experimented with a few reforms of his own, such as allowing some private businesses to open and allowing farmers to sell some of their crops on the open market. He did not want to defy the Soviet Union, which was still Cuba's economic lifeline. But Castro truly believed that the path of reform could only spell the end of communism.

EIGHT

The Special Period

As his country's international influence and economic future grew more uncertain, Castro responded by becoming more despotic. In 1989, he had one of his top military generals, Arnaldo Ochoa, arrested on spurious charges of treason and drug trafficking. Ochoa's real crime had been criticizing Castro for his leadership during the war in Angola and for his neglect of veterans who had returned from fighting wars in Africa. Ochoa was court-martialed on television and executed by a firing squad. The reaction sent a clear message of how dangerous it was to challenge Castro.

Castro was heartened for a few days in August 1991 when Communist hard-liners led a coup in the Soviet Union against Gorbachev. However, the Soviet people took to the streets in fierce protests and soon brought Gorbachev back. By the end of the year, Gorbachev had resigned and the Communist Party was out of power. The Soviet Union, for most of the twentieth century the world's dominant Communist state, was no more. It broke up into the independent countries of Russia, Ukraine, and a number of other states. Russia's new president was the reformist Boris Yeltsin, who made it clear Russia would no longer be Cuba's economic lifeline.

The Soviet Union had for years been buying Cuban sugar at a high price and shipping cheap oil in return. The end of this agreement spelled an energy and economic crisis in Cuba. Agriculture, industry, and trade dropped and much of the country sank into poverty. For a time, Castro's regime looked to be on its last leg. Sensing that Castro was weak, U.S. president George H. W. Bush signed the Cuban Democracy Act in 1992, tightening the U.S. embargo on Cuban goods in an effort to finish him off.

Castro responded to the crisis with a series of emergency measures known collectively as the Special Period of Time in Peace. Cuban agriculture had previously been run using industrial equipment dependent on a steady source of oil. Castro moved to revert to more primitive methods of cultivating crops. Food and other commodities were rationed.

Castro tried to encourage tourism, which brought both money and problems. Tourism earned $250 million in 1994, a figure that reached about $2 billion in five years. As tourists flooded the country, they also demanded goods and services. Educated Cubans, such as doctors and engineers, abandoned their work to drive taxis or wait on tables because tourism paid more money than their regular jobs. Many women even turned to prostitution.

Hoping to ease the unemployment and discontent, Castro announced another open emigration policy in 1994. About 30,000 Cubans sailed for Florida in all manner of craft; many died in the crossings. Prior to the surge, the U.S. government had accepted any Cubans arriving on U.S. soil without a visa because it considered them refugees. But now that Cuba encouraged emigration, the U.S. government balked at admitting huge numbers. After negotiations between Cuba and the U.S., the two parties

A boatload of refugees leave Havana in 1994. They named their boat The Hope. (AP Photo)

agreed to a "wet feet, dry feet" policy in 1995. If U.S. authorities picked up a Cuban immigrant at sea on his way to Florida ("wet feet"), he would be sent back to Cuba or to another country. If he made it to shore ("dry feet"), the U.S. would let him stay and petition for asylum.

During the 1980s, some observers had speculated that Castro was grooming his son Fidelito to succeed him. In 1984, Castro had appointed Fidelito as chairman of Cuba's Atomic Energy Commission. In 1992, however, Fidelito abruptly resigned. Several years later, when a U.S. journalist writing a book about Castro asked him about Fidelito's resignation, Castro replied that Fidelito had actually been fired.

A map of post-revolution Cuba. (University of Texas)

Although Castro remained intensely—almost fanatically—private, other personal matters found their way into the press. In 1993, his daughter Alina, who had remarried and given birth to a daughter, falsified a passport and left Cuba for Madrid, Spain. She later moved to the United States where she now hosts a Miami talk show and has become one of her father's biggest critics.

Although he was having internal troubles in the 1990s, Castro managed to alter his world image. He continued to denounce U.S. policies in his speeches, but he sounded less quarrelsome. Even those countries that were staunchly anti-Communist started to view him as a fairly reasonable leader, moderate enough to engage in meaningful dialogue. In most quarters, sympathy for Cuba grew.

Relations with the United States also seemed to be on the mend. In 1995, Castro's government arrested Robert Vesco, a U.S. fugitive. Vesco had fled to Costa Rica in 1973 to avoid charges of stealing over $200 million from a Swiss mutual fund and funneling illegal contributions to Richard Nixon's political campaign. Vesco had lived in Cuba for some time until he was arrested for a scheme involving a fraudulent cancer and AIDS drug. At first, the Clinton Administration thought Castro might send him back to the United States for trial, but Vesco remains in a Cuban jail.

Just as tensions were easing between the two countries, trouble resurfaced in 1996. On February 24, Cuban fighter planes shot down two private aircraft operated by Brothers to the Rescue, an anti-Castro group of Miami-based Cuban exiles. Both pilots died. The planes had dropped anti-Castro literature on Havana just before the attack. The United States claimed the planes were in international airspace, but the Cubans claimed they were over Cuba. Castro, for his part, declared that they would not have been shot down if the pilots had heeded warnings to leave. "We are not to blame," he said. "We did not want anything like that to happen."

Shortly after the incident, President Bill Clinton signed the Cuban Liberty and Democratic Solidarity Act (better known as the Helms-Burton Act), which strengthened the U.S. embargo against Cuba. The act denies a visa to anyone who has profited from property seized during the 1959 revolution, restricts the movement of Cuban diplomats on U.S. land, and increases the broadcast range for Radio Martí, an anti-Castro radio station supported by the U.S. government. Most importantly, it allows the U.S. to impose sanctions on foreign companies that do business with Cuba. The European Union, Canada, Mexico, Argentina, and other groups with trade relationships with Cuba denounced the Helms-Burton Act; so did humanitarian groups, claiming that U.S. sanctions punish the people of Cuba, not its leaders.

The 1990s also saw changes in the relationship between Cuba and the Roman Catholic Church. Castro began to negotiate with Vatican officials about a possible papal visit. Castro knew the strength of the church's fight against communism in Europe, but he could also see that a visit by the head of the world's Catholics could only enhance his own stature as a world leader. Pope John Paul II, meanwhile, saw the trip (the first time a pope has ever traveled to Cuba) as an opportunity to reinvigorate the Catholic Church in Cuba and shed light on some of the suffering there. He demanded that the government not tightly control his visit.

John Paul II visited Cuba in January 1998. He celebrated mass four times in four different locations, the last time in Havana at the Plaza of the Revolution. He met with Castro and Cuba's religious leaders. Castro played the role of the welcoming, gracious host. He gave holidays to government workers so they could attend the papal events. The pope criticized the U.S. embargo and spoke of how Western consumerism can have corrupting effects on the poorer countries of the world. This, in particular, pleased Castro, who often harangues against the consumer society. The pope was not entirely complimentary, however. In several speeches he called for human rights and more individual freedom.

The pope was not the only one to criticize the U.S. embargo on Cuba. Every year, the General Assembly of the United Nations overwhelmingly passes a resolution calling for the U.S. to lift sanctions on Cuba. But the embargo was, and still is, highly popular in parts of the U.S., particularly among the politically active Cuban exile community in Miami that zealously opposes Castro. Because of its solid stand and influence in the politics of a major state, the exile community exerts what some feel to be a disproportionate sway on U.S. politics. Florida is a critical battleground state in presidential elections.

Those who support the embargo believe that lifting it would condone and support Castro's rule in Cuba. Its opponents point out that the U.S. has normalized trade relations with a number of other former adversaries, such as China and Vietnam. In fact, experts have long argued that the U.S. embargo hurts Cubans but helps Castro. Castro is able to blame the United States for Cuba's faltering economy.

A year after the pope's visit, a new episode incited friction between Cuban immigrants in the U.S. and the old regime. It began on November 25, 1999, when young Elián González was found floating in an inner tube in the Atlantic Ocean off the coast of Fort Lauderdale in Florida. A raft carrying Cuban migrants, including Elián's mother, had capsized, and she had died. Elián was the only survivor.

The U.S. Immigration and Naturalization Service (INS) put Elián in the care of his relatives in Miami, who said that was his mother's wish. But Elián's father, divorced and remarried, lived in Cuba and petitioned for the boy to be returned to him. In January 2000, the INS ruled that Elián should be returned to his father. The ruling set off mass protests in the Cuban community in Miami. The Florida Family Court reversed the INS decision, only to have that reversal overturned by U.S. attorney general, Janet Reno.

Through the next months, the Elián González case filled the courts and national newspapers. Lawyers for Elián's relatives in Miami fought the U.S. government's decision. Finally, on April 6, Elián's father and his second wife

This billboard in Havana during the Elián González crisis reads, "Return Elián to his Homeland." (AP Photo)

arrived in the United States, and federal officials ordered the relatives in Florida to surrender the boy. When they refused the INS made a predawn raid on the house where the boy was being held. Federal agents whisked Elián from the home of his relatives and reunited him with his father in Washington. The raid caused riots and street demonstrations in Miami but on June 28, 2000, the U.S. Supreme Court rejected the appeal of the boy's relatives. Elián and his father returned home to Cuba.

Castro took advantage of the incident. Throughout the affair, he claimed that Elián had been kidnapped, and should be returned to Cuba. Thousands of Cubans took to the streets, calling for Elián's return. After Elián was returned, Castro attended the boy's birthday party and his graduation from the first grade. Several times he called Elián up on stage with him at events for the Cuban Communist Party. The opportunity to be filmed joking and interacting with a six-year-old was a public relations coup for him in Cuba.

In 2001, Castro was nominated for the Nobel Peace Prize. A left-wing member of the Norwegian parliament, Hallgeir Langeland, said he endorsed the nomination because of the Cuban leader's work toward helping developing nations. The nomination was controversial and Castro did not win. The 2001 Peace Prize went to UN secretary-general Kofi Annan.

In 2002, Jimmy Carter, the former U.S. president who would win the Nobel Peace Prize for that year, became the first U.S. president to travel to Cuba. Carter called for better relations between the two countries. He spent five days in Cuba, during which time he received the red carpet treatment. He met with Castro three times, attended a baseball game, was the guest of honor at two state dinners, and met with various other officials, including anti-Castro dissidents. Perhaps most dramatically, he spoke to the Cuban people in a nationally televised event. In the address, Carter called upon the United States to be the first to ease the tension by lifting the trade and travel embargo. At the same time, he asked the Cuban government to allow free speech in Cuba.

President George W. Bush was not happy with Carter's visit and speech. Bush owed a large part of his election victory to the Cuban-American, vigorously anti-Castro vote

Fidel Castro, Cuba's revolutionary leader during the late 1950s, is still a major player on the world scene in the twenty-first century. (© Agência Brasil)

in Florida, which had been invigorated to vote Republican by the Elián affair. His administration stood firmly against Castro. Shortly after Carter returned home, Bush announced there would be no easing of the embargo. Instead, he sought to tighten travel restrictions to the island.

During the early years of the new century, Castro established diplomatic ties to Hugo Chávez, the anti-American leader in Venezuela. A career military officer, Chávez was elected as Venezuela's president in 1998. Chávez has loudly and vigorously denounced U.S. economic policy and has worked to drive a wedge between the U.S. and other nations in the region. In Venezuela, Castro has found a close ally to supply Cuba with cheap oil. The support has helped to finally lift the Cuban economy out of its post-Soviet era crisis.

Castro has defied the world's two major superpowers during his long career, but even he cannot stop the march of time. In June 2001, he was giving a characteristically long-winded speech at a rally outside of Havana. Thousands of spectators listened intently as he ranted for more than seven hours under the broiling sun about terrorist groups from Miami who were planting bombs and plotting against Cuban leaders. Then he fainted. Paramedics revived him in the ambulance, but Castro insisted upon returning to the platform to tell the audience he would continue his speech later that evening. Three years later, Castro fell off a stage after giving a speech at another rally, breaking his knee and his arm. He appeared on Cuban television only moments after the fall to reassure the public that he was fine.

Castro is now over eighty years old and the only leader many Cubans had ever known. There is a great deal of speculation about what will happen to Cuba after he is gone. Officially, his brother Raúl is his successor, but Raúl is only four years younger than Fidel. Indeed, Raúl, who is said to drink a bottle of Scotch whiskey a day, may be in even worse health than Fidel.

Raúl is the staunchest of Communists in the hierarchy of Cuban leadership, but he has neither the political insight nor the charisma of his brother and it is doubtful he could keep the country in line. However, as armed forces minister, Raúl is in control of most of Cuba's military. In the event of a struggle for power after Fidel's death, Raúl would surely have the upper hand. It is highly unlikely that anyone in the leadership of Cuba's Communist Party would dare challenge him. If Raúl succeeds Fidel, Cuba will probably continue much as it has for half a century—at least for a while. But once both Fidel and Raúl are gone, no one can say what course Cuba will take.

Castro has ruled his country for more than fifty years, outlasting ten different U.S. presidents. Observers have been mistakenly predicting his death or downfall for years. He is still on top of events in his country. When Hurricane Dennis hit Cuba in 2005, he was there in a television studio checking on the storm's progress and extent of damage. In August 2005, in his annual birthday speech, he offered no hints of retiring. Castro's doctor predicted that he would live to be 120 years old.

In late July 2006, however, Castro fell ill and needed surgery for intestinal bleeding. While recovering, he ceded power to his younger brother and constitutional successor, Raúl. It was the first time Castro relinquished power since he took office in 1959.

Castro's legacy is uncertain, but he can certainly point to an improved standard of living, better health care, and higher literacy for millions of Cubans. However, the economy has foundered on his watch. Many observers have likened his domestic rule to that of a medieval king. He has ruled his country directly and authoritatively, acting at times with great benevolence and at other times with shocking disregard for basic rights and freedoms. More so than perhaps any other world leader in the modern era, he is the government of his country, and he has not instituted any sustainable system that will persevere after he is gone.

On the international stage, Castro's achievements are equally debatable. He has not led the Third World to communism. In the late 1980s, the Marxist regime in Ethiopia collapsed and in 1990 the Sandinistas fell from power in Nicaragua. Years of civil war have dramatically weakened the MPLA in Angola. Yet the recent rise of several leftist leaders in Latin America, including Hugo Chávez and Bolivian president Evo Morales, might indicate a decisive turn to the left in Latin American politics.

Regardless of whether Castro is remembered as a bold nationalist who stood up against the United States or as an eccentric, brutal tyrant, he is unquestionably one of the defining figures of the twentieth century.

timeline

1926	Born on August 13 in Oriente Province, Cuba.
1932	Attends La Salle school, Santiago.
1935	Attends Dolores Jesuit school, Santiago.
1942	Enters Belen Jesuit school, Havana.
1945	Graduates, enters University of Havana to study law.
1947	Joins group in abortive mission to overthrow Dominican Republic.
1948	Goes to Bogotá in April for student conference, participates in urban riots; marries Mirta Díaz Balart on October 12.
1949	Son Fidelito is born.
1950	Graduates with law degree.
1952	Starts grassroots campaign in bid for congress; Fulgencio Batista seizes power in military coup.
1953	Leads unsuccessful attack on Moncada Barracks to overthrow Batista on July 26; sentenced to 15 years in prison.
1955	Released from prison in general amnesty; joins brother Raúl in Mexico; meets Che Guevara.
1956	Sails to Cuba with band of revolutionaries; retreats into Sierra Maestra.
1959	Batista overthrown on January 1; Castro enters Havana to take over Cuba on January 8.

1960	Signs major pact with Soviet Union; sends aid to Algeria; United States begins partial economic embargo.
1961	Cuba-U.S. diplomatic relations are severed; anti-Castro exiles, backed by CIA, are defeated in Bay of Pigs invasion; Castro declares Cuba a socialist state.
1962	Cuban Missile Crisis; U.S. imposes full trade embargo.
1963	U.S. bans its citizens from traveling to Cuba.
1964	Cuban fishing boats captured by U.S., released after paying fine.
1967	Castro supports Warsaw Pact invasion of Czechoslovakia; Che Guevara killed in Bolivia.
1972	Cuba formally becomes a Communist state; Castro visits Guinea and Algeria.
1974	Sends aid to Angola.
1977	Sends troops to Ethiopia; U.S. drops ban on travel to Cuba.
1979	Elected chairman of Non-Aligned Movement; approves Soviet request for aid to Afghanistan.
1980	Mariel boatlift in which some 125,000 Cuban refugees flee to U.S.
1983	U.S. invades Grenada in October.
1989	Cuba signs 25-year treaty with Soviet Union.
1990	Soviet Union collapses.
1992	U.S. passes law against sending food and medicine to Cuba.
1994	Declares open immigration policy; thousands of Cubans flee to U.S.
1996	Cuba shoots down two planes from exile group in U.S.; Helms-Burton Act tightens restrictions on Cuba.
1998	Pope John Paul II visits Cuba; Elián Gonzalez crisis.
2000	U.S. lifts food and medicine ban.